Angels
Guides
&
Other
Spirits

Incredible Events
From The Unseen World
Around Us As Told By A
Spirit Release Therapist

JOYCE PETRAK, DCH

Angels
Guides
&
Other
Spirits

**Incredible Events
From The Unseen World
Around Us As Told By A
Spirit Release Therapist**

JOYCE PETRAK, DCH
("Dr. Joy") Doctor of Clinical
Hypnotherapy

Cover: Psychic Artist, Ida Marie
Interior Portraits: Psychic Artist, Elaine Regis

IMPORTANT MESSAGE

Neither the author nor publishers are medical doctors and make no claims to the medical effectiveness of Spirit Release Therapy. This book is for educational purposes only. The author does not answer medical questions. Proper care by a certified medical doctor should be sought immediately if there is sufficient cause to use a physician. This book is not to be used for diagnosing, treating or prescribing for any illness.

Original Edition: Copyright 1996 by Joyce Petrak, D.C.H.

Curry-Peterson Press
Post Office Box 839
Lenoir City, TN 37771

ISBN: 0-9633177-1-7
Library of Congress: 96-096875

Dedication

This is the Angels' book and they have often struggled to make sure it gets out. Thanks to Angels, Guides and Other Spirits for their love, dedication, inspiration and determination. May you receive in love the messages that they wish you to understand.

Thanks to Holy Spirit, Jesus, Mary, my Guardian Angels and Spirit Guides (especially Simon) for their continuing love and assistance. I love you.

A special thanks to all my human helpers: Barbara Phillips, my precious Office Assistant; Mary Alice Miller, for editing; and Dr. Joyce Kruger for improving the book with her unyielding corrections. Blessings to Jean Bedard of Happiness Communications and Tom Dorow at BookCrafters for seeing the book into final form.

And last, but never least, to my best friend and patient, supportive spouse, Bob. I love you.

Contents

viii ❖ ❖ ❖   *Angels, Guides & Other Spirits*   ❖ ❖ ❖

CHAPTER 6   Fire! Fire! Get Out!   **96**
*A crisis solved with Angel help that leads to puzzling
questions. Introducing Johnna and Angel Samora.
Channeled: Surprising answers to some ancient
mysteries.*

CHAPTER 7   A New Kind Of Spirit   **115**
*Bringing Dr. Phil to Balbir. Samora speaks;
then David, a higher entity. Finally, a dramatic
introduction to George, a high-healing Spirit
from a different galaxy.*

CHAPTER 8   Soul Rescue In Vietnam   **132**
*Balbir accepts a spiritual assignment
to help thousands.*

CHAPTER 9   Different Methods & Protection...   **143**
Including "Do It Yourself"
*How other practitioners help earthbound souls.
What you can do.*

CHAPTER 10   Dolphins, Whales & The Environment   **154**
*How Angels and God's "lesser creatures"
help the planet to survive.*

CHAPTER 11   Are These The End Times?   **166**
*Latest predictions from channeled sources
about what to expect, and what to do, during
the next few years.*

CHAPTER 12   Saving The World — & Ourselves   **194**
*It's easy. Go into the Silence. Find out what some
advanced souls have said about deep prayer.*

NOTES   **211**

BIBLIOGRAPHY   **217**

INTRODUCTION

Is It Or Isn't It?

*F*iction? No... but a little, yes. Names, dates and some locations have been altered to protect privacy. Some events, which happened separately, are put together.

This is the amazing story of one group of my students who started in what was to be a two-month class in *Spirit Release Therapy*. They were also to learn basic hypnosis, re-birthing and regression to "Heal the Child Within."

The experiences that happened to the seven (and to the teacher) were so profound that the class continued for several months. Some still meet at times. As graduates, they are simply called *Soul Workers*. With Angelic assistance, they are now helping millions.

Before telling some of the events in their lives, however, you need to understand a little about the spirit world as we now perceive it. It is unbelievably vast and, perhaps, could be compared to knowing about all the different animals and their sub-species that exist in our world.

A few spirits will be explained and historical references given so that you won't believe all this was just made up. It has not been an easy journey to accept some of the following and I have often been surprised (stunned) at what I was learning. I have had several years to absorb the ideas contained here. You are getting much of it in one book. So, please fasten your seat-belt for an exciting journey.

If there are parts that do not fit in with your belief system, just read on. It is better to consider the information as fictional than to lose your inner peace. Realize that the material in these chapters is my perception of what I heard, saw and was told. Listen to your own inner spiritual guide to see what is right for you.

– Joyce Petrak, D.C.H.
"Dr. Joy"

CHAPTER 1

Ghosts, Attachments & Things That Go Bump in the Night

*E*ntities? Attachments? Ghosts? You must be kidding. Precisely my thoughts when I was first introduced to these concepts by Dr. William J. Baldwin in May of 1988. Dr. Baldwin, D.D.S., Ph.D. of Enterprise, Florida, is the author of *Spirit Releasement Therapy: A Technique Manual*.[1] He is the country's leading teacher on how to release attached spirits from a living human.

These are the basic premises of *Spirit Releasement*: When people die, their bodies are left behind and they become spirits or soul entities. Many look up and pass through a dark tunnel on their way to a bright light. This has been documented by many who have had a near-death experience (NDE). Others return from a NDE without remembering this happening to them.

Theologians say God gave us free will. It appears there is never a time when this gift is taken away. Time is meaningless in the spirit world and there is no rush to get anywhere. There is no giant vacuum which sucks us up to "Heaven" or "Higher

Planes" at death. Souls have a natural instinct to go toward a "Light," but the upward direction is not always understood by those recently deceased. Their thoughts, their emotions remain down on earth and this is where they stay until they are spiritually helped to make the transition toward "The Light."

This *must* be their first step. Whether they then go to a last judgement, as many believe, or to rest and then learn according to their abilities, as others suggest, is not the point at this time. For now, we are concerned with "Earthbounds," spirits who have remained on earth.

Unattached, these entities are considered ghosts or haunting spirits. For comfort, or a feeling of safety, or because they are drawn to the light of a person's aura or magnetic field, many of these spirits attach themselves to a living person. About the size of a firefly, they are much like a parasite. Some leave at will, but the majority seem to think they are stuck, or they don't want to leave and do not try to free themselves.

Entities usually transfer the anxieties, fears, anger and pains which were present at the point of their deaths to their host when they attach. The living person can then feel all kinds of unexplained emotions, pains, skin conditions, fears, mental confusion and, sometimes, a sense that an inner voice seems to be speaking to him/her.

Phobias, panic attacks, bouts of anxiety or depression can also torment the living. An unwarranted sense of loneliness or sadness can be present. Humans with spirit attachments may have bursts of anger or even violence. There can be a feeling of rejection or alienation. "This just isn't like me," they may say or feel. These unfortunate possessed ones may be unable to control the use of alcohol, drugs, food, sex, etc.

Obviously, not all of the above afflictions can be attributed to spirit attachments. There may be many other reasons for such phenomenon. However, there are an amazingly high number of problems which can and do have their source in discarnate beings. Hundreds of therapists, especially well-trained hypnotherapists, have discovered that spirits do often remain earthbound and can, and do, influence human beings.

Admitting this spiritual reality to a skeptical scientific community is quite another matter with a therapist who wants to keep a job or who makes a living through referrals. One of the first brave souls to come out with her findings was Dr. Edith Fiore, author of *The Unquiet Dead... a Psychologist Treats Spirit Possession.*"[2] Her book has become a best seller. In it, she reveals that she has found hundreds of cases in which attached entities have caused psychological, and even physical problems for her clients. After Dr. Fiore helps the spirits to leave, many of the client's problems usually disappear.

To achieve depossession, a therapist assists a client into entering a deeply-relaxed state. The person is encouraged to visualize a time or place where they were once especially happy and then to relive the experience in their mind. Then, with the client "gone away," it is possible for the hypnotist to communicate with the spirit attachments who are now able to talk through the relaxed one. The entities may speak in a low tone, using the client's own voice or, the voice may change dramatically. Various accents, child-like voices and inflections — which were decidedly not the client's — are often heard.

After speaking gently to the spirits for awhile, they are encouraged to look up. They *always* see "the Light." It may be grayish at first or seem far away "like a star." It becomes brighter as they continue to look at it. They may express surprise that it was there. "How does the Light feel?"

"Peaceful," "Loving," "Happy," are often the answers.

There are other times when the answer is not what I want

or expect. When I asked one male attachment, "Did you ever look up and see a bright Light?" he responded, "Yeah, I sure did and I saw my mother coming. She's dead! I don't want to be near no ghost. I'm not looking up! I like it here."

"Did you every think that maybe you could see her because you're a spirit, too? What's the last thing you can remember when you had a body?" I questioned him gently.

"Oh, I dunno. Let's see. Yeah, I was coming home late and these two guys jumped me. I put up a big fight, but they must have knocked me out because I don't remember how it ended."

"Charlie, you're staying with Mark right now. How did that happen?"

"Well, I was just wandering around. I guess I was confused after being hit on the head. There was a light by him and he seemed real pleasant. Probably I was looking for someone to be with for protection. I just sorta decided to hang out with him and not be any bother so he'd let me stay. Isn't that okay?"

At this point, I had to help Charlie understand his true situation. "Charlie, I must tell you something important. You died in that fight. You have an eternal spirit and that's what you are in right now. YOU don't have a body. You are attached to Mark's body and that's not okay. You need to go to heaven. Do you know anything about God?"

"Ah, well, not much. I didn't guess He'd want to see me."

"Charlie, God created you. He loves you like a son and wants you to come home."

Charlie had trouble digesting all this strange news, but I didn't give him much time to think about it or argue. "Your mother still loves you, too, Charlie. I know you love her. That's why she came to get you. She wants to take you home. Look up now! See that beautiful Light?"

"Yeah, it looks real nice."

"Keep watching it, Charlie. It will continue to get brighter. Look now and see if someone is coming and don't be afraid."

"I see someone. Can't make out… oh, it's Ma! She's holding her arms out to me! Is this real?"

"Yes, Charlie, it's real. Feel her love and ask her what she wants with you."

"She's come to take me home to Heaven. Can I go with her?"

"Yes, you can. Go with our love and give our thanks to your mother for coming."

At this point, there is generally a joyful reunion and tears may be streaming down my client's face. Each situation is different, but in the end, they all leave happily.

Prayer for spiritual and Angelic help precedes each session of *Spirit Releasement*. After thanking God for allowing us to do the work, we call on the needed Angels, including asking Michael the Archangel to keep out all darkness. If the client is Christian, this Christian therapist can ask for the help of Jesus. For a non-Christian client, this can be done silently. In the end, it is the Angels who have been given the task of bringing the earthbounds "Home to the Light… to Heaven." Entities are never allowed to go alone because they might easily get lost again. The heavens are vast.

As Dr. Fiore found, a client's life generally improves dramatically even after a single session. Other therapy is frequently called for in subsequent sessions as a person is freed from possessing influences and gets in touch with "the real me."

I like to do at least two follow-up sessions. The first is to "heal the child within." The adult client visualizes him or herself taking care of the younger self at a time when the child was gravely upset. Normally, with hypnosis, we can take care of three to five situations in an hour. During the next session, I ask the subconscious to take the person to a time and place he/she needs to know about to gain insights to improve present-day life. The subconscious responds with images that are amazingly vivid and helpful. Each session is extremely powerful for a client.

As a spiritually oriented therapist, I was intrigued when I first heard about these concepts, but frankly, I didn't believe them. It was just too bizarre. However, something inside me insisted that I HAD to take Dr. Baldwin's class. I did and the direction of my life took an amazing turn. It has been an exciting adventure working with what some call "the most important healing work on the planet."

Of the more than one thousand people with whom I've worked since my first introduction to *Spirit Release Therapy*, only THREE did not seem to have any attachments whatsoever!

I am often asked, "Does that mean I have attachments?" My answer: probably, but everyone is different. I allow two to three hours for a session. Some are easy. Some are almost impossibly difficult, but the results are always the same. ALL the spirits go toward the Light; back to their Creator…to God. What happens then is vague, but I find TOTAL consistency in the results from the releasement.

How is it possible for souls to attach? I can only explain it this way: our body is not the real us. We are an eternal spark of God consciousness. A firefly is the best visual example I can think of. Like the firefly, this spark encompasses our mind, soul, personality and whatever else that remains when the body dies.

Our bodies are home to millions of parasites, from tiny mites to bacteria to other things which we don't like to think about. I picture the body as being like a giant loaf of bread. When loose spirits attach to it, they are like raisins in the loaf, just more parasites. The spirits often attach themselves to those who are weakened from illness, fatigue, depression or the negativeness of anger, resentment, fear, guilt, etc.

After a Sp*irit Release*, when all the attachments have been removed, convincing a client that what was was seen, felt or heard (often all three) was real is sometimes difficult. They may say, "I must have been making that up. It couldn't really have happened… did it?"

"How do you feel now?"

"Well, I feel… I feel LIGHTER!" is most often heard. "It's like someone just took a load off my shoulders. Gee, it feels great! But was it *really* happening?"

To convince clients of the reality of their experience, I make a cassette tape of each session. However, I encourage them to wait a couple of days before listening to it so that they can first mentally process what they remember. "You'll know by reliving the session that it was definitely real," I tell them.

One really left-brained accountant, who wept like a baby when it was discovered that his deceased wife was still with him, later said, "I can't logically believe this happened. On the other hand, I can't deny my emotions. I haven't cried this way since the day she died."

While he was in a hypnotic state, it had taken me a long time to convince the wife that she would be happier in heaven and that she was harming her husband by staying. After expressing her love for him, she finally left with an Angel. Before her death, she had been severely depressed. She apparently brought this emotion with her when she attached to her husband because he had been seeing a psychiatrist for many months because of his own deep depression. After his Sp*irit Release* session, he was no longer depressed and was able to lead a normal, happy life. He did come in for the two additional recommended therapies, but the main problem had been solved.

As the therapist, I am only a vehicle through which *Spirit*

Releasement happens. The Angels do all the important work. Angels, I was amazed to find, come in a huge variety of unique personalities and with different abilities and assignments. They will be discussed in later chapters. Now, for clarity, we will first focus on explaining how and why some entities choose to attach themselves to humans.

The real "us" is an eternal spark of God consciousness which is temporarily lodged in a body. Leaving the body, we become a spirit, or ghost, and may choose to remain on earth for awhile. Since eternity is some billions of years, there is no immediate hurry to decide.

The word "ghost" originally meant "spirit" or "soul." So, the Holy Ghost was the name given to the third person in the Trinity of God. To "give up the ghost" meant to die. This was understood to mean the person was no longer on earth. His spirit or life force was gone from the body and was never to be seen again. With the passage of time, however, a "ghost" came to be understood as a haunting or earthbound spirit. They are spirits who had not decided to rise heavenward toward a bright, magnificent Light. There is no time in the spirit world and free will is *always* honored. So, even after death, a soul can still choose.

However, over 4,000 years of ghost stories have resulted in these disembodied spirits having nothing to show for their efforts but laughter, derision, disbelief and, generally, bad press. Looking at it from the ghosts' perspective, it is extremely annoying to be ignored and misunderstood. In fact, few people are even aware of them. Of course, animals — cats and dogs especially — always seem to know when there is a spirit around. They may howl, run in fear or, if the spirit remains in their building, they may get used to it and, eventually, even ignore it.

Although often shy about discussing it, hundreds of clients

have told me of being aware that a recently departed spouse, friend or relative has visited them. Sometimes once, sometimes many times. They may have felt frightened, or they may have had a sense of peace about the visit. Often they admit to having sort of a conversation with the spirit and sensing a response. It is less common, but some "see" an apparition or ghostly movement.

When spirits remain in a building, such as their home, and are detected, the house is considered haunted. This can result in a quick succession of owners. If spirits become increasingly annoyed at strangers in their house, they may try to scare the live ones out. The process for getting ghosts to leave and go Heavenward is different from that of working with attachments to a human, since we can't usually talk directly with them. Some spirits convey thoughts to a person willing to do automatic writing and a good psychic may be able to mentally communicate with them. However, getting them to leave with the Angels still requires prayer. Whatever method of communication is used, it is always to be done in a loving way. They are not to be treated in an adversarial or antagonistic way. Please remember that these spirits, too, are children of God.

Soul Travel

Information about the journeys of the soul has been found in esoteric literature and teachings for centuries and, in recent years, has become more clearly understood. Also, the Near Death Experience (NDE), previously mentioned, in which a soul goes through a tunnel toward a bright Light and is then told to return, is now the subject of many books, articles, movies and TV shows. Those who have this experience no longer fear death and their lives are often dramatically changed.

Without a NDE, people experience soul travel or leaving

the body in other ways. For instance, I knew a helicopter pilot whose extreme fear of death was interfering with his work. So, he began to pray about it. One night he had a dream: while flying his helicopter, he suddenly encountered a mountain looming up in front of him. In a panic, he desperately tried to avoid hitting it, but he violently crashed. As the wreckage plummeted toward earth, he became aware that he was floating. As the pilot calmly watched the scene, he felt no fear and a peaceful feeling gradually enveloped him like a soft blanket. As he continued to drift, the sense of peace deepened so much that he was totally overwhelmed by it. Shortly, he awakened and was disappointed to realize that he had been dreaming.

"I've never had such a magnificent feeling in my whole life," he enthused. "I was so frustrated when I woke up and it was all gone. I know this was an answer to my prayer and I'll never fear death again. I know now I'm here for a purpose and, when my life ends, I expect to enter a truly beautiful world."

If the next world is so great, why are spirits earthbound? There are many reasons: fear, love for those grieving, confusion, anger, unfinished bushiness, etc.

Some of these were observed in the popular film, *Ghost*.[3] It was considered humorous science fiction by many, but others understand that there is a great deal of truth in the movie. In *Ghost*, when the hero was murdered, his spirit runs after the fleeing assailant for about a block. Suddenly, he realizes something is missing… his body. Totally confused, he returns to the fallen corpse where his girlfriend is screaming for help. The hero's spirit accompanies her to the hospital where he becomes frustrated in his attempts to communicate with her. After the doctors tell her that there is no hope of reviving him, she returns home completely distraught.

Out of compassion, he stays with his grieving love even

though she is unaware of his presence. Gradually, he understands that he is dead and accepts the fact that he is a spirit. Soon after, he becomes aware that she is in danger from the murderer and his accomplice. As he realizes that his death was not a chance shooting, his energies go toward saving the girl and forcing the killers to trap themselves.

As the film unfolds, the hero discovers he can go through walls and do other things only a spirit can do. He meets another earthbound — a violently angry spirit who is capable of hurling objects around. Seeing the possibilities, he refuses to leave the angry one until he can learn how to move things. This involves some difficult and, at times, humorous attempts until he gets the hang of it by directing his mental energies.

With his new capability to move objects, he brings the killers to justice. The young woman accepts the presence and identity of his spirit and understands that his love transcends death. In the poignant ending, the spirit hero realizes his work is done and, as a bright Light grows ever stronger around him, he knows "it is time to go." At the end, he walks into the Light.

The film illustrates clearly why most spirits are quiet while others slam doors, move objects and, in one of our cases, played the piano at night. Some earthbounds are smart enough to figure out that they have powerful minds. Because of boredom, anger, frustration or other feelings, they begin to experiment. They often just want attention. They may be genuinely sorry that they cause panic with their antics. Or, perhaps, it may amuse them.

The movie also showed several of the reasons spirits stay earthbound. The first was that he didn't realize he was dead. Eventually, he caught on, but it is amazing how many don't seem to understand this rather obvious fact. If souls are spiritually ignorant, they can become confused after death because they have no comprehension of their situation. How can someone

NOT know they're dead? It is difficult to believe, but a goodly proportion of souls are either into denial or in a sleep-like state and feel they are dreaming.

When I realize they may not know they are dead, as in Charlie's case, I gently tell them. I'm often met with disbelief. "I'm stunned," replied a young soldier who had been killed many, many years before and had to be told the news of his demise. Although the interests of the living client are the main concern, it is sometimes necessary to do therapy on a spirit.

The dead man in *Ghost* returned to his apartment to be with his girlfriend and because he didn't know what else to do. This is a common occurrence. Spirits frequently return to their homes and may stay there for hundreds of years. Many haunted homes and castles are witnesses. This seems to happen often if a person was murdered.

This has been accepted in Europe for many centuries. Shakespeare's *Hamlet* is about the ghost of his murdered father appearing to him. Hamlet's father wanted an injustice righted, as did the hero in *Ghost*. Modern, scientific, left-brained people have been told it is ignorant to believe in ghosts or other spirits. So *Hamlet* and *Ghost* are just entertainment, with no real substance. But, as Hamlet said, "There are more things in Heaven and earth, Horatio, than are dreamt of in your philosophy." (Act 1, Scene V)

There are several reasons why souls do not go to the Light.

SUDDEN DEATH. Those who are killed or die suddenly, such as in an accident, can be angry and frustrated. They do not understand that they are dead and are upset because no one pays any attention to them. If a man dies in battle, he may still be violent as he fights his enemies.

GETTING LOST. Another common reason is the confusion from feeling "lost." Children who die in accidents, for instance, may still be looking for parents. "Why did you come to stay with Mary?" I asked one spirit child.

"She had a kind face and reminded me of my Grammy," was the reply.

These young souls get very excited when they feel the love of the Angel who has come to take care of them. They sense they are going to a beautiful place where there are lots of others to play with. At times, a close spirit relative is allowed to come from Heaven to bring them to their new home.

FEAR. Fear is another big reason why souls choose to stay on earth. Some are aware of not having led good lives and are afraid of going to a condemning judgement. When they express sorrow for past deeds, they are delighted to look into the eyes of an Angel and know it has come "to take them home." Other fearful spirits are hiding from someone who wanted to hurt them. They do not realize that their attackers can no longer reach them.

MATERIALISM. People who were totally immersed in the material world in life may only be conscious of wanting desperately to finish whatever they were involved with. After their death, this could lead them to eventually inhabit the body of someone they feel they can influence. They would then try to control this person in order to get them to carry out their wishes.

THE HELPER. Sometimes it is difficult to convince spirits to leave a human. Their reasons can actually be somewhat noble. "If I leave, they'll walk all over her!" insisted one spirit who felt it her duty to "protect" the lady she was inhabiting.

ADDICTIONS. If a person dies while addicted to drugs and/or alcohol, the spirit usually still craves the sensations of the substances abused. These addicted spirits may hang out around bars or street corners and, when patrons are high on something, their aura — the energy field which protects them — is weak and the entities can dive in. This is one reason it is so hard for many to quit an addiction. Spirits inside of them are constantly prodding them to fulfill their own urges. If an addict dies, all the entities must quickly leave. They cannot stay without a life force. They look for someone new and the process continues.

Solving the many problems caused by earthbound attachments requires new and enlightened thinking on the part of therapists, clergy and humanity in general. The common religious understanding about possession is that it is when people have demons in them. Most of the demonic force, or fallen angels, have never had a human form. They are exceedingly clever about hiding, and it is usually only after all the formerly human spirits leave, that it is possible for Soul Workers to locate them.

Dr. Fiore alludes to the demonic in *The Unquiet Dead*, but does not tackle that aspect of this unfamiliar process. Dr. Baldwin, my teacher, acknowledges learning much from Dr. Fiore, but he is acutely aware of demonic possession and treats it as a separate part of the "cleaning out" process. He teaches this part of *Spirit Releasement* in his classes. (The demonic is explained in Chapter 3.)

Dr. Baldwin also feels there are many other things which can inhabit a human, such as soul fragments, elves, fairies, etc. In my work, I found one claiming to be a leprechaun. I can't confirm that identity, but I found him quite charming. Eventually, he went to the Light as any other entity would. I have also dealt with extraterrestrials and, while I consider most of those visiting earth to be friendly, these particular ones were NOT the good guys.

RELIABLE HISTORICAL SOURCES

While the idea of earthbound spirits may be new to most, it is definitely not new historically. Following are a few references to them from various ages.

George W. Meek spent 50 years traveling widely and investigating all that was known about life after death before coming out with his book, *After We Die, What Then?*[4] in 1980. He reports that for over 2,000 years, history has recorded references to "demons."

In ancient Greece, both Plato and Socrates were aware of spirits. Plato held that demons obsessed mortals. Socrates speaks directly of demons influencing the insane. Plutarch wrote: "Certain tyrannical demons require for their enjoyment some soul still incarnate. Being unable to satisfy their passions in any other way, [they] incite to sedition, lust, wars of conquest and thus get what they lust for."

The Old Testament recounts that "David took a harp and played with his hand. So Saul was refreshed, and was well, and the *evil spirit* departed from him.[5] Later, Minucius Felix, a Roman, wrote in Octavius: "There are some insincere and vagrant spirits, degraded from their heavenly vigor... who cease not, now that they are ruined themselves, to ruin others."

So common was the knowledge of spirits and spirit possession in the time of the first Christian apostles, that the ability to cast out evil spirits was considered one of the most important signs of discipleship. Many of the healings accredited to Jesus involved removing spirits. Current New Testaments translate "spirits" as "demons," those under the rule of Satan.

In more recent times, we have vast volumes regarding spirits of all kinds from the amazing Emmanuel Swedenborg (1688 to 1772), who lived in Sweden. He wrote about 17 different sciences, some of which he discovered and developed.

His original contributions were in fields as diverse as anatomy, astrology and paleontology.

In 1743, at the age of 56, Swedenborg claimed he experienced a "visitation" in which he was able to converse with spirits and Angels. He abandoned his scientific work and, for the next 30 years, immersed himself solely in spiritual meditation and medium-like trances. He claimed to have talked to biblical prophets, apostles, Aristotle, Socrates and departed friends as well as spirits from other planets. While he wrote about heaven, hell and Angelic beings, he saw his main mission as being scriptural interpretation to clarify and enhance spiritual understanding. Thirty large volumes resulted, many of which were dictated to him and written while he was in a deep meditative or trance state.

During this time, Swedenborg also studied all that was then known about the mind. He also examined his own dreams. Delving into the inner reaches of his psyche, he discovered the spirit world and vividly described these beings. He claimed that some of the spirits he saw and conversed with were of high intelligence while others had only a minimal understanding of things. They certainly sound like the earthbound attachments that many therapists are now finding. He may have been the first one to write about how spirits can attach to the living.

Swedenborg became quite clairvoyant as a result of investigating the spirit world, but never showed signs of instability or mental disturbances during his everyday life. However, he was treading on dangerous ground for the eighteenth century. He was writing about things which were considered the sole concern of religion. That is, the clergy. Since he revealed information not considered accepted teachings, there was a clerical uproar and, eventually, he was tried as a heretic. Although Swedenborg was not convicted, his reputation suffered and he did not make public his subsequent writings.

This battle resulted in furthering the strong wall which was slowly separating doctrine which was considered "science" and that which was "religion." Eventually, there evolved an unwritten agreement to stay out of each other's turf. Unfortunately, with a few brilliant exceptions, science and spirituality have largely ignored each other for over two hundred years. This resistance to the holistic mind-body-spirit model is the main difficulty with helping therapists of all kinds to understand spiritual healing work, such as *Spirit Releasement.*

Fortunately, more and more professionals and laity now understand that there is an unbreakable link between mind, body and spirit. With quantum physics, vibrational healing, energy balancing and numerous other enlightened approaches, science and spirituality are inching toward each other. It will take more time, but truth is an uncompromising teacher.

SPIRITUALISM

After Swedenborg, there was not much overt interest in spirits, attached or otherwise, until near the end of the 1800s when Spiritualism developed. It evolved from some spiritually-gifted people who met and began to gather in small groups. Eventually, they attracted a large following. There have always been people like this who were gifted with clairvoyance or "inner sight." In the past, you could be declared a witch and burned at the stake because you saw spirits, *knew* about the future or knew things about others that they hadn't revealed. Even now, many are afraid to discuss their spiritual gifts and try to suppress what they "know" and "see." In our "enlightened" age, I still hear people speak about churches or groups which they consider "from the devil" because the people have spiritual gifts such as prophecy, clairvoyance, faith healing, praying in tongues or clairaudience (clear hearing).

Spiritualists realize that all gifts which are used with prayer and for the good of others are from God. Many are clairvoyant and can distinguish and communicate with spirits. Some are much more gifted than others and can see earthbound spirits who are attached to a human or to their aura. The Spiritualists pray for help and protection and are able to talk to spirits and help many earthbounds "go to the Light."

Their methods are not as therapists as they do not *need* to converse with a possessed person. Sometimes, they "see" from a distance and can work for releasement even if the person with attachments is nowhere near.

DR. WICKLAND

Before the end of the 1800s, perhaps inspired by the Spiritualists, Carl A. Wickland, a medical doctor, was having some astonishing experiences. His wife proved to be a superb deep trance medium and she would allow her voice to be used by an obsessing entity who was attached to one of Dr. Wickland's patients. By talking to earthbound spirits in this way, he was able to explain their situation to them and encourage them to leave his patients and go "home" toward the Light.

After three decades of this work, he wrote *30 Years Among the Dead*[6] in 1924. His insights and information are invaluable to therapists and anyone interested in spirit work. Because of great demand, his book was re-issued in 1974.

At his sessions he had a "psychic circle" of volunteers to pray for and be supportive of the spirits. They prayed for spiritual help. The Angels who came to assist they called their "Co-workers." The doctor's methods resulted in excellent success in curing many mental patients as well as people with other problems.

His book is the earliest source I've found to warn people against Ouija boards. Many cases of possession have been attributed to this "game." Dr. Wickland wrote: "The serious problem of alienation and mental derangement attending ignorant psychic experiments was first brought to my attention by the cases of several persons whose seemingly harmless experiences with automatic writing and the Ouija board resulted in such wild insanity that commitment to asylums was necessitated."[7]

Dr. Wickland tells about an amiable, pious and refined woman who suddenly became boisterous and noisy while shouting obscenities and romping around. She insisted she was an actress and had to dress for the stage. Eventually, being completely irresponsible, she had to be committed. Through his wife, Dr. Wickland was able to get the possessing dead actress to leave and go to the Light. Shortly after, the cured woman went home.

He writes about another dignified lady who became violent and ran around screaming, "God save me!" She would rush into the street and kneel in the mud, refusing all offers of help. In another case the police had to be called for a woman who was violent and presumed herself to be Napoleon. Dr. Wickland was able to help these ladies also, but he noted that all had been using Ouija boards.

It is true that many have used the boards as a game with no problems. Becoming involved with spirits that you don't know can be most risky, however, and there are safer ways to have fun. The young girl in *The Exorcist* film supposedly got into her predicament because she was using a Ouija board. "Burn them!" seems to be the best advice. Even if a spirit does not take you over, it could be giving some very bad advice.

As Dr. Wickland wrote: "Death does not make a saint of a

sinner, nor a sage of a fool. The mentality is the same as before and individuals carry with them their old desires, habits, dogmas, faulty teachings, indifference or disbelief in a future life."[8]

In the cases of possession mentioned above, which were rescued by the Wicklands, there were the prerequisite prayers for protection before starting a session. The doctor wrote: "She [his wife] is constantly protected from the invisible side by the supervision of a group of strong intelligences known as 'The Mercy Band,' which is guiding this work, endeavoring to bring humanity to a realization of the simplicity of the transition called death, and the importance of a rational understanding of what becomes of the spirits."[9]

Dr. Baldwin, the *Spirit Release* authority, acknowledges the value of Dr. Wickland's book and research, but warns against letting a spirit of any kind actually possess a person. He said, "Sometimes it is easier to get spirits in than it is to get them out. If you are working with a person who is a good channel, make sure that any spirits speaking through the person are told, in no uncertain terms, that they may speak through the channel, but under no conditions, may they possess him or her."

Dr. Wickland saw such dramatic improvement in his patients that he wrote these strong words, "The influence of these discarnated entities is the cause of many of the inexplicable and obscure events of earth life and of a large part of the world's misery."[10]

Can we really attribute much mental illness and many of the world's problems to these lost spirits? If so, rescuing these earthbounds actually is the most important healing work on the planet.

Dr. Wickland also wrote about "War Neurosis" or shell shock. He felt that many returning soldiers were possessed by the spirits of dead comrades who were not aware of their transition. He wrote: "This neurosis is indicated by delirium, hallucinations, anxiety states, paralysis, functional heart disorders, tremors, gait disturbances, convulsive movements, pain, anesthesia, blindness, speech disorders, etc."[11]

Dr. Baldwin has also discovered ex-soldiers with attached spirits as the cause for their problems. After *Spirit Releasement* and follow-up therapy, their symptoms and phobias disappear. He feels the potential for helping troubled soldiers with this type of therapy is limitless.

Dr. Wickland was writing about ex-military after World War I. The possibilities, or know-how, to help them through *Releasement* has not been used since then (to our knowledge).

GUIDES

In addition to the immense assistance received from Angels, there is tremendous help available from Spirit Guides — that is, those who lived on earth, died and went to the Light. After souls go to Heaven, they rest and are taught many spiritual truths. Then, they have options. One is to return to earth occasionally in spirit form, to assist and guide humans. They are not lost, like ghosts, but wish to help out of love and to advance their own spiritual life. They are never allowed to interfere with another's free will or possess them. But, if someone is open to guidance, help is available.

For instance, if a person prays for help in figuring out a mechanical problem, a Guide may be sent. They are in line with Divine will, just as Angels are. God doesn't actually come down and assist. He/She makes use of the billions of helpers who were created. A mechanical problem isn't something you probably want Angelic advice on, especially when there is a Master Mechanic in the Heavens somewhere who would be happy to help. Guides, like Angels and all of us, each have their own job or specialty, just as in a large (VERY big) corporation.

Dr. Wickland was given much information from Guides. Usually they were spirits who had been helped to the Light through the efforts of his "psychic circle." After the required time in Heaven for them to assimilate spiritual understanding, they came back at times to thank the Wicklands and their group. They then shared some of their knowledge, speaking again through Mrs. Wickland.

One spirit who was helped returned because his wife assisted in the Prayer Circle. She was delighted when her husband returned to speak. After blessing her and telling of his love, he said to the group:

> *This world is only a school where we gain understanding through experience. In the spirit world we go on and on, progressing closer to God. But before we can progress, we must have an understanding of spiritual laws. If we have not the right understanding, then we remain in darkness and hover around the earth plane.*
>
> *I am pleased that I had even a little knowledge of the higher life, for when I reached there, my spiritual eyes were opened and I could see and realize the beauties of the spirit world.*
>
> *I have met many of my dear friends on the spirit side of life. Many whom I knew are still in darkness and I have tried to help them understand their transition. [Another job Guides are allowed to do.]*
>
> *If I could only express the conditions on the spirit side of life so that you would get the full meaning! There is such beauty, such harmony.*[12]

Despite Dr. Wickland's vast collection of information, there was little heed paid to this entreaty: "Advanced intelligences on the invisible side continually urge that broad-minded investigators on the physical plane cooperate with them in establishing research centers in asylums, churches, universities and other institutions."[13]

Like Swedenborg, Dr. Wickland was ahead of his time and his research languished even though many prominent citizens gave endorsements. On the back of the title page of his book, this appears from Sir Arthur Conan Doyle, of Sherlock Holmes fame, who was an avid Spiritualist: "I have never met anyone who has such a wide experience of invisibles. No one interested in obsession or the curing of insanity by psychic means should miss this book."[14]

In spite of a few profit-hungry charlatans who tried to profit from the Spiritualist movement, it grew in popularity and size. Some highly-gifted people amazed the crowds. Then, Dr. Wickland's findings were published and many serious investigations were made. The validity of many Spiritualists was confirmed, often reluctantly. Dr. Wickland had many enthusiastic believers, but the medical establishment would never endorse him.

The Catholic church also started a serious investigation of all the activities regarding spirits. For centuries their clergy has worked with exorcisms and they have developed a lengthy ritual of prayer and command to demons to leave a person and return to hell. However, their understanding was only of Satan and his minions. Their devils had had no bodies and these claims of attached spirits were something quite new.

Dr. Godfrey Raupert of London, who was especially delegated by Pope Pius X to lecture on Spiritualism to Catholic audiences in America, said in substance:

> It is no longer possible to put the subject of psychic phenomena aside. Scientific men all over the world have

recognized spiritism as a definite and real power, and to shelve it as a dangerous policy.

Consequently, the Pope has asked me to tell Catholics the attitude to take toward the subject... The Church admits the reality of these spiritistic phenomena and their external intelligences. In fact, it has always admitted to their reality. The problem at present is to discover the nature of the intelligence. We are now on the borderland of new discoveries which may revolutionize the world. It is not the time yet for an explanation of all the phenomena. We must suspend our judgement until the subject is better known. The study of spiritism is a new one and therefore dangerous... A partial knowledge of the subject may cause grave dangers [resulting in obsession or possession].[15]

It seems that nothing further was ever publicly announced about the study. People may have forgotten about it as they were caught up in all the "new discoveries" of telephones, railroads, autos, flight and the vast number of Edison's inventions. Spiritualism remained alive (and is so today), but it was never accepted into the mainstream of religions or into their joint activities.

These short explanations of ghosts, attachments and Spirit Guides should prepare readers for some of the work now being done. The more one works with the spirit world, the more one understands how much more there is to learn. The knowledge and information is as vast as the Heavens. Only a tiny fragment can be put into any book. What *Soul Workers* do know is that, as the Wicklands discovered, the Angelic and Spiritual world is MOST anxious to assist humans in any way they can.

Their main interest is in our spiritual growth and enlightenment, but they respect our human needs and often help us in the most mundane ways. They want us to have a spirit of joy, happiness and wonder which comes with a deep sense of inner peace. Working with Angels is an exciting journey. Join the fun!

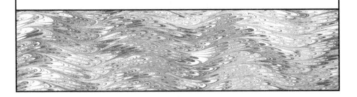

CHAPTER 2

Talking To Angels & Guides

Prayer for Protection

*The Light of God surrounds us; the
Love of God enfolds us; the Power of
God protects us: the Presence of God
watches over us; Wherever we are,
God is and all is in Divine Order.*

— JAMES DILLET FREEMAN

"*How* did you start talking
to Angels?" I'm often asked. Well, it wasn't something I was
comfortable with for a while, I assure you. As a therapist, I wasn't
trained to ask clients, "Have you talked to your Angel lately?"
In fact, it didn't seem prudent.

The first conversation started in my office by "accident"
when an Angel signaled me. (A person in a light hypnotic state

is conscious of what is being said, but is so relaxed, it is a chore to even talk. So, I teach them to signal by lifting their finger. The index finger signals "yes," the thumb indicates "no" and the little finger means "I don't know" or "I don't understand.")

I had finished working with a client earlier than usual and was wondering if I could give some additional help. Suddenly, I heard myself saying, "Does this person's Guardian Angel wish to talk to him? You may signal me."

To my great surprise, the index finger immediately shot up in a "yes" signal. "Thank you, Angel. What would you like to say?" I then asked.

A soft, gentle voice began speaking through my client and gave him an inspiring message. It was far more insightful than anything I could have said and was delivered in tones of the greatest love and compassion. The voice knew this person at a VERY deep level. If the message had come from my client, he would have spoken in the first person and said, "I want you, etc." But this voice addressed him by name several times and gently helped him to see situations in a new and spiritual light. After a while, the Angel said, "That is all for now. I am glad to help you whenever you call on me."

I was so dumbfounded that I could only stammer, "Thank you. Ahh... thank you for coming."

I sat quietly for a moment until I recovered from this Angelic visit. I then brought my client into wakefulness. We both exclaimed, "Wow!"

During the post-hypnotic discussion, I inquire about what the client observed and felt. I also want to make sure the person is wide awake and well grounded before going out to drive a car and talk to others. When people come out of an intense trance, after being deep into their sub-conscious, they are often "space cadets."

In the above case, the session had been helpful to my client, but the words of the Angel had made the greatest impact. "He *really* knew me," he exclaimed several times. "And what he said was so logical. It really helps clear up so much. Oh, thank you, Dr. Joy."

"That wasn't me. That was your Angel you need to thank. And I think he wants to talk to you some more. You need some quiet time when you can just listen." The gentleman inhaled deeply as he realized that his busy schedule was going to have to allow this important business in.

Following this, my first Angel encounter, I occasionally asked if the person's Angel wanted to speak. Sometimes, the signal was "no," but more often it was "yes." When an Angel spoke, the words were usually so profound and uplifting that I could only marvel.

Being enthused about these Angelic contacts, I told a small group I was training in *Spirit Release Therapy*. They immediately asked to try and see if they could contact their own Angel. The students had been taking turns being in the hypnotic state while the others observed. At the end of their session, I now began to ask if their Angel wished to speak. Most did. When we got to Kathy, her Angel was quite different. She addressed the group rather than Kathy and said that she was not a Guardian Angel, but a "Soul Worker." She had come because that's what the group was about and she wanted to assure us that this was a most high calling for which the heavens rejoiced. The Angel said that because we were willing to do this work, we would always be protected by St. Michael the Archangel's helpers and would have all the Angelic assistance we needed. She cautioned, however, that we must never start our work without prayer. It was essential that we always be conscious of the need for prayer and for asking for Angelic assistance and protection. God would bless our work, but we must be aware that it was serious and important and not take it lightly.

We all felt overwhelmed and extremely humble. When our new helper was through speaking, she asked, "Are there any questions?"

Ask an Angel questions? Oh, my, what a thought. However, in all my life I have never been without questions, so I timidly asked, "May we know who you are?"

"Yes, of course. I am an Angel devoted to helping souls reach Heaven, or the Light, as you say. We have no names, but you may call me Athena. And, now, God's blessings on you. I must leave."

Athena… a name known throughout history as the goddess of Wisdom. How appropriate. In our marveling and talking with each other after she left, we almost forgot about Kathy. When she awoke, she was quite dazed, but kept saying, "Oh, my! How beautiful. What pure love. It was wonderful!"

Kathy was always a most loving soul and shone with an inner beauty. We used to tease Kathy that she hugged everything that moved. Sometimes when complete strangers came, they were startled when Kathy would go up and give them a beautiful, loving hug. It was not surprising that Athena had come through this warm, caring person.

After this initial encounter, we became quite familiar with Athena and were never again timid about asking questions. In fact, at the end of talking to us, she sometimes laughed and said, "Now, Joy, I know you MUST have questions." And, of course, I did. If you can get answers right from a heavenly source, there are certainly LOTS of things we humans want to know.

By the time the group finished training, I had discovered that Athena could assist with many of my clients. Kathy began coming to the office quite regularly to help with difficult situations. For instance, a man was concerned about his wife who had had a stroke. She could barely talk, but Athena was able to see the woman's soul with her spiritual eyes and, with our request, remove some attached entities that were causing the woman to behave strangely.

Kathy is able to sit down and put herself into a deep meditative state. After about three to five minutes, Athena is there and greeting us. Her voice, mannerisms and vocabulary are decidedly not Kathy's. In fact, there is enough of a physical change in Kathy that I often welcome Athena before she speaks. This amuses her and our conversation is soon relaxed and casual, like old friends talking.

One time, when Kathy wasn't in the office, I had a young man who came because he was positive he had attachments. However, he was so nervous that he could not relax and, in spite of my best efforts, he would frequently open his eyes and get up and pace around. With about 95% of the people, I'm able to get them to relax. However, there are always a difficult few whom I can't help.

In this case, I called to see if Kathy was home and could help. She was available and happy to assist. After going to a quiet place, Athena came through. We were separated by about thirty miles, but that seemed to pose no problem for an Angel. It took some time, but eventually, the young man was "cleaned out" from entities, including some very nasty ones.

This was when we first learned that people need not be present for us to work on them with Angelic help.

One time we had a woman ask for assistance for a niece in England about whom she was concerned. This was new for us and we asked Athena if she could help with someone that far away. She smiled patiently and said, "Of course. You must remember we have no space or time in eternity." I felt like a little child whose parent had to keep reminding her of something over and over. I knew that it had been written of since St. Augustine in the fifth century, but most humans find it really difficult to accept the concept that there is no time or space in the spirit world.

We were able to connect with the woman's niece with no difficulty and find the source of her problem. Since then, we are often asked to work on someone from a distance.

As time went on, Kathy had family obligations which kept her from participating regularly. It was always a joy when she came, however, and at times she and I would get together just to get information from Athena. We would have her help us with our loved ones or with people about whom we were especially concerned. One night, when asking questions, I suddenly wanted to know: "Athena, could I channel?"

"If you wanted to," she replied.

I thought this over for a minute and then said, "Yes, I'd like to. What should I do?"

"Just what Kathy does."

Great, I thought, Kathy gets to just lie there and let an Angel come through. That seems easy enough. Then, I felt completely unsure as I realized that I would have to get "me" — my ego — out of the way. I had always been the teacher, asking the questions, writing down the answers and making sure that the tape recorder was turned on at the right time. How was I going to get myself out of the way? Well, it would be worth a try.

"Okay, Athena, I really would like to channel." I said. I then woke Kathy from her hypnotic state and showed her how to work the tape recorder. We traded places and I settled into the big recliner. We repeated the prayer for protection and then, I added, "I allow my voice to be used by a spirit from the Light who comes in the name of God, if this is Divine Will. Under no circumstances is any other spirit allowed to speak through me or to possess me. Thank you, Angels, for coming with your love and protection."

Then I laid back and started taking some deep breaths. I imagined myself on a beautiful beach and tried to feel the warm sun and hear the call of the seagulls.

It was almost immediately that a strong masculine voice came through me and, speaking in a British accent, said, "Ah, good evening. I'm Simon. I've been waiting to talk to you."

SIMON SEZ

I can't remember anything Simon said that night, but he made a lasting impression on Kathy and me (and anyone he has talked to since). Whimsical may be the best way to describe him although, "What a character!" is what I hear most often as people laugh and shake their heads. They marvel at his knowledge about them and his deep insights. The admonitions Simon gives to people are said in such a gentle and Puckish way that no one can take offense. He loves to laugh and could almost be called a spirit of joy as he gets people to lighten up on themselves.

Simon is decidedly not an Angel. He is a Spirit Guide who is a Master Teacher and loves helping others. He has not had a body in well over 300 years, so he has had plenty of time to increase the vast amount of knowledge he acquired when he was on earth. Whenever I try to get information about his life when he was here, he dismisses it with, "That's not important, my dear. We must work on the here and now."

However, over the four years I've channeled him, Simon has slipped on several occasions to reveal things. Actually, he probably didn't "slip" at all, but likes to tease me with a little tidbit of information every now and then. For instance, I was part of a panel about Angels on a Detroit TV show where the co-host was John Kelly. As we walked into the studio, I heard him say telepathically, "My name was John also."

"Oh, it was John?" I mentally asked.

"Yes, but I like Simon Sez," was his reply. "You know we just have vibrations and not names in the spirit world. So, I can pick what I want. Don't you think Simon Sez is fun?"

"Oh, it's just great. Whatever you say," was my resigned reply.

When Simon first talks to someone, he usually communicates with their Guardian Angel who tells him something about the person's childhood. This establishes that Simon is talking with a spirit who REALLY knows this one. (A Guardian Angel stays with a person from the time of conception until he/she returns to the Light.) Simon then tells the person something that I couldn't possibly know so that he or she is confident that the information isn't coming from me.

Simon usually starts out talking about the person's Guardian Angel. Since each Angel has its own personality and abilities, they are all quite different. Most often Simon gives a name for the Angel... usually a feminine name for women and a masculine name for men. "A woman might feel embarrassed in the shower with a male Angel hanging around," Simon says laughingly. "Of course, they are just spirits, neither male nor female. But humans have trouble with that concept."

Most often, the name will have some sort of personal significance.

Simon then gives guidance about the person's life and helps them to understand things more clearly. When he finishes, he says, "Now, do you have a question, my dear?" (or Sir if he's talking to a man).

This is a surprise to the person who usually has trouble thinking of a good question unless I warn them beforehand. Simon is mainly interested in the spiritual life of those he advises, but often he helps them with a personal problem, or with a concern for someone they love.

"I am not a psychic and what happens depends upon the free will of several others," Simon usually replies to inquiries about the future. Once, when we asked him about the earth changes and when to expect the major shifts that have been predicted, Simon was patient, but seemed to feel that we should be advanced enough not to need to ask.

SIMON: *There are millions of Angels and other spirits working with earth now to stabilize things as much as possible, so it won't be too traumatic for the masses. But there are still many who need to come up in their spiritual consciousness: their Christ consciousness, if you will. They are the ones desperately needed to help with this whole Ascension process, this spiritual uplifting in which mankind understands all are one in God.*

So many who should be helping are still totally engrossed in their own little lives, their personal successes and failures. They do not understand that once they agree to work for mankind, all their needs will be met. As you know, God will never run out or money. Naturally, people need to be practical and prepared for what it is they are supposed to do. This often takes time. We are putting people into the right places as quickly as we can so that they can teach others. There are some who need patience until we can help them get into the right situation or the right place.

Dr. Joy: That's clear. But we are still wondering if these dates we keep hearing about earth changes, etc., mean anything?

No, because of free will. We have no way of knowing exactly when everything will be in place. Only God knows that. In the meantime, all the spirit world is working unbelievably hard to pull off the most spectacular events earth has ever seen. We keep saying it will be soon because we see most of the pieces in place. Exactly when, we choose not to guess. We don't want you to become involved in worrying about it. You will be wherever you are supposed to be. Your job is to continue learning through meditation, reading and helping others. You need only work on yourself. Not perfect yet, are you? No, I thought not. Well, just keep working on your need for self-discipline and to grow in love. That's a big order right there.

Remember, the Spirit world isn't worried about the time because they don't know about time. They just do their job with love. That's all we expect of you. Clear?

Yes, Simon. Very clear.

When people ask Simon about a relationship problem, he is usually helpful. Several times he has been questioned about breaking off a romance, marriage or situation involving children or peers. "If you continue with this person, will you be able to grow mentally and spiritually?" he will often question.

If the answer is no, Simon asks if the other person is retarding their growth, perhaps controlling or stifling them. If the reply is affirmative, Simon might say, "You are on this earth plane to learn, to grow, to become closer to God. Your classroom is here. Holy Spirit is your Teacher. Your obligation is to see that He can get through to you. For that to happen, should you leave this relationship?"

At this point, the person can usually answer their own question. There are times, however, when the client indicates a need for one more nudge when they say, "But I feel so responsible for him [her]."

To this Simon gently suggests, "Give this person to Holy Spirit. Every time you think of them, send them Love and Light. Continually pray that Spirit will bring them the right human teacher. You know that isn't you, don't you? They must find their own path. When you throw out the negative vibrations of worry, you are actually harming the person. Give them to Holy Spirit to take care of and just be trusting while you pray and send Love and Light. Don't — I repeat DO NOT — take back what you have given to Spirit by worrying again. Just say, 'Thank you, God, that this is taken care of.' Remember, all healing starts with gratitude." People usually leave Simon with a far lighter heart.

Several have come to ask him about a loved one who is deceased. He asks how long the person has been gone and what is the first name. Then he says, "Wait a minute until we get a messenger Angel to find the soul. Just think about the person so that the Angel can pick up the vibration."

After about a minute, the word comes back and Simon says something about the person that would identify him or her, such as: he always wore a hat; she's wearing a big apron; he seems to be dancing, etc. Once the client confirms the person's identity, Simon lets them know if the person has come back from the Light with words of love. Or, if the deceased is still resting and cannot come, Simon relays that they are happy to be remembered and they send love.

Sometimes the spirit is still earthbound. With the client's permission, Angels come and the deceased is told to look up to the Light. He or she is helped to understand it is now time to go. A great deal of love is always exchanged and, frequently, tears.

For one distraught mother whose son died at twenty-one, Simon said, "I see he was a remarkable young man. He brought a great deal of joy to you and others. Did he not?"

The mother answered, "Oh, yes, he was wonderful to everyone who knew him."

Simon then gently said, "He did the work he came here for. It may have been brief, but it was all he was supposed to do. He cannot be completely happy, however, as long as you are grieving this way. You have a choice, mother. You can now rejoice that your son is happy in heaven and constantly thank God for the joy He gave you by sending this wonderful son for twenty-one years. Or, you can be bitter and miserable and make yourself ill by bewailing the fact that he is no longer here. What is your choice?"

It took some time, but eventually, the woman realized she did have a choice and she decided that she wanted to make her son and herself happy.

Often I notice that Simon does not tell a person what to do, but asks them questions which, by their answers, helps make their situation clear so that their answer becomes obvious.

Simon has helped hundreds now, including my husband and myself. When we have questions or concerns, we invite Simon in for a chat. It is a casual, light-hearted dialogue like you might have with an old and dear friend... which he is. The difference is that, along with the levity, Simon has some profound thoughts, and at times, very amazing ideas. We always have a lot to think about after a visit with Simon. He has added a wonderful dimension to our lives, in addition to being a delightful friend.

Simon loves to tell people about their Angels and Guides and helps them understand that through meditation they can learn about and develop a wonderful relationship with their closest friends. For Christians, this great friendship can also be developed with Jesus. I have even talked to Jews who felt Jesus was very personal and considered Him an elder brother.

Simon usually arrives within a minute after I ask for him. After the *Prayer for Protection* is said, he is soon present. Once, he was so anxious to talk to a certain person that he popped in before I had finished the prayer and completed it for me.

Another time, he took quite a while in arriving. "I thought you weren't coming," I thought mentally and he replied, "Oh, sorry. I was on another planet watching some most fascinating experiments. This is one of the great advantages of being in spirit form. You can roam all over the universe. It's so interesting. But now, I'm here. How can I help you?"

Having a Spirit Guide with a sense of humor can be a lot of fun. He enjoys laughing and he likes American slang and phrases. He uses them whenever he gets a chance, but not always the way we would. Sometimes people don't get his British humor.

Often, when people first encounter channeling, they are rather stunned. A voice from beyond, scary and serious stuff, they feel. Then Simon starts talking, just as casual and friendly as can be. It sometimes takes a while before they can loosen up and enjoy the experience. What's more, Simon wants a dialogue. At first they may not realize this and Simon will have to ask them a question or, "Is it not so?" a couple of times before they understand that he expects their response.

Even the Angel Athena admits that Simon has helped her to be less serious and we find she is now throwing in some of her own light humor. She readily concedes that it has come from being with "her good friend, Simon." It was also Athena who let us know that Simon has LOTS of friends all over the universe. "Oh, nearly everyone knows Simon," she told us. "He's quite a gadabout."

It has been through our exchanges with our spirit friends that we began to understand that humans and Angels can form friendships in Heaven and they don't look on each other as being "different." Truly, all is Love and Harmony in God's domain.

Having come from a structured and conservative religious background, it is not surprising that I began to have doubts about this channeling business. Was this really from God? Were the Angels and Guides I heard totally in line with the will of God? I began to seriously pray about it.

One method I use for getting answers is to pray and then open the Bible. On two different occasions, I did this. Both times I got readings about King David. The first was 1 Samuel, 23:2, "So he consulted the Lord, inquiring, 'Shall I go and defeat these Philistines?' The Lord answered, 'Go, for you will defeat the Philistines and rescue Keilah.'" Further down, in verse 4, "Again David consulted the Lord, who answered...." And, in verse 11, "O Lord God of Israel, tell your servant. The Lord answered..."

King David himself was not only inspired, but often called on the prophets and oracles. It seemed to be assumed that God was going to give him and his people answers to their problems. Now where were they getting their information from? Not from God directly because God just is. "I am Who am." He has given His Angels charge over us and they are His messengers. So David and the prophets obviously received messages from Angels or Guides. If God allowed these messages to come to His appointed people in ancient times, why would He not continue this throughout all ages? God equally loves ALL His people and He is the same today for us as He was for those in past centuries.

Some are not channels that spirits speak through, but they hear an Angel or Guide (or devil) in their mind. A lady called me up one time and asked, "How can I talk to my Angel?"

"How are you talking to me?" I answered. "You can't see me; you've never met me; but you know I'm talking to you."

It's true, however, that you must test the spirits. If you are Christian, ask: "Do you come from the Light in the name of Jesus?" Asking "From the Light" is important because a well-meaning earthbound might feel it was coming "in the name of Jesus," but would know it hadn't come "from the Light."

Non-Christians might ask, "Do you come from the Light in the name of the one true God [or Allah, Jehovah or however they refer to God]?" It seems spirits are compelled to tell the truth and devils simply can't say they came from the Light.

After you have communicated with your Angel and/or Guide for some time, you will recognize your channel immediately and will trust the voice. It will be like getting a call from your best friend or a close relative. You immediately recognize the voice and a certain inner vibration and there is no need for identification. In my own case, I usually hear my Angel in my right ear and Simon in my left.

People who "hear" God speaking to them may hear His messengers, but one must be very careful and TEST. Many heinous crimes have been committed by people who later said, "God told me to do it." A true Angel or spirit understands this and is patient while you test to your own satisfaction. Don't worry about taking up their time. They don't know what "time" is.

So, what about the admonitions to stay away from "mediums?" This warning was given in the Old Testament to a nearly barbaric people who were not very advanced, spiritually nor intellectually. Because they wouldn't have known how to test spirits, there was a concern that they might be conversing with earthbounds. King David, however, seemed to have been quite sure to whom he was talking. So, too, did Mary, the mother of Jesus. She talked to an Angel, as did the father of St. John the Baptist.

For a couple of years, I began to hear channeling from many places. Once again I began to have my doubts, so again I prayed and opened Scripture. Again it was about David, only in 1 Chronicles 14. Here we also find David inquiring and God answering. After the reading, I heard my Angel: "Are we not from the Light? Don't we aid with good and spiritual information to help you grow in love for God and man? Be not of little faith."

Since then, I have humbly accepted channeling as another beautiful gift from God.

If we are open to Holy Spirit and are listening, there are MANY, MANY channels these days. Angels have told us that there are more than a billion additional Angels who have been sent to earth to help mankind in our Ascension process, that is, raising our spiritual consciousness. There are now numerous articles and books that have channeled material. There are also channeled cassette tapes available. A *Course In Miracles* is channelled as are most of the articles and artwork in the inspiring magazine, *Connecting Link*.

Ida Marie, our cover artist, is not only a psychic artist, but has an "inner knowing" which allows her to help many. Elaine Regis, another psychic artist, drew the pictures of Athena, Samora, David and Simon which are illustrated in the book. She has those who come for pictures of their Angels or Spirit Guides sit for her as if she were drawing their own portrait. After prayer, it is as though an unseen hand directs her hand and a drawing begins to appear. Working in pastels, it takes her an hour or two to produce these beautiful pictures. Elaine has no formal art training.

Music is another area where there are inspired artists. Those who have heard the Angels sing, say there is nothing on earth to compare with the magnificence. However, many spiritual musicians are producing inspired works that are truly thrilling. These are all great channeled gifts as are some sculpture and other artistic forms.

There are now pictures and statues of Angels everywhere, including note papers, greeting cards, posters, and U.S. stamps. People wear little Angel pins on their shoulders. One interior decorator told me that it was just a fad and that it would be over in a short time. She wasn't open to hearing anything else, so I just mentally blessed her and continued on my way. Not everyone is ready for Angel information. Nor should anyone be pushed on the subject. It will only make them turn away. Free will must be respected.

When I encounter someone persistent in telling me that everything I'm doing is from the devil, I just smile and say, "Bless you for your love of God and your faith. I'm sure you are very sincere in your beliefs, but they are not the same as mine." Then, I release it and let it go. I found it unwise to argue and try to match wits. I surely would have in the past, but my Angel has led me to see things differently. If people have a strong faith in God, it is not my job to alter their belief system. God loves them just the way they are.

The Holy Spirit's voice is as loud as your willingness to listen. It cannot be louder without violating your freedom of choice.

– A COURSE IN MIRACLES
page 145 of the Text

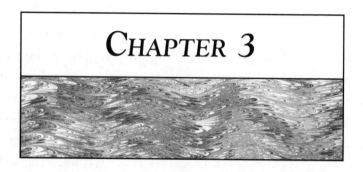

CHAPTER 3

I Talk To The Devil...
It's A Cold Day In Hell

It is definitely not fashionable to talk about the Devil in most circles. Well, yes, all the dreadful things that are happening are disgustingly evil, but that must be the result of a chemical imbalance in the brain. What else could it be?

But the Devil? Well, he's just a scary figure for Halloween costumes. He is an anachronism; that is, he's ancient history, "one from a former age that is incongruous in the present" (Webster's dictionary). Getting widespread belief for this thinking may be Satan's greatest act of cunning.

As a *Spirit Release Therapist* who has talked to hundreds of demons who spoke through the vocal chords of my clients, I can testify that SOMETHING is certainly there. These beings have called me some interesting names that usually only come from the sewer. I know they are NOT earthbound spirits because they have never had bodies; they do not comprehend time and they become terror stricken when I suggest they might have to go back to their master and admit failure. If they have refused to listen, this last point nearly always gets their attention.

Demons, like Angels and humans, each have their own personality. Controlled by Satan, they are in army-like ranks from powerful generals down to the "grunts" whom I usually call "the little ones." There are probably millions, perhaps billions, of them. Most seem quite stupid, but are capable of being really irritating. These small demons are dark, blob-like, genderless characters. They are rarely found without supervision and may be little higher than a thought-form. It is easy to get their attention, but they dare not leave the human they are attached to without an order from their commander. They fear and hate him, but are afraid to go with the Angels until they are certain that he is tightly secured and can't get at them. They are delighted if they can escape.

The general belief is that Satan (or Lucifer, which means Light Bearer) was a member of the Seraphin, the highest order of Angels. The usual Scripture interpretation is that when Satan got angry about something and wouldn't obey God, he was driven from Heaven with a third of the Angels, who were his followers. Since then, with the aid of the fallen angels, he has endeavored to get the souls of humans to join him in hell.

There are many different viewpoints surrounding this belief, such as: it is the Devil's job to let humans see how horrible evil is so they will turn back to God and no longer be separated from Him. Though people have a great capacity for pain, sooner or later they realize, "There must be a better way." When they open their minds, they allow the Holy Spirit to gently lead them back to God. This can happen even after a person's death since the soul retains free will and can eventually choose to be out of the sorry state they are in.

Numerous other theories exist, but it is not my aim to present them here. It is only necessary to understand that there are many opinions about how the demonic came to be. My work is to let people know that great numbers of demons do exist and explain how to deal with them. I believe that freeing people from possession of any kind is rescue of the highest order and enables them to again live their lives in complete control. This frees them from some forms of mental illness or neurosis or just from nagging temptations, insatiable desires or anti-social behavior. This is a goal of *Spirit Release Therapy*.

Since ancient times, there have been Exorcists of one kind or another throughout the world. A large number of Jesus' cures were attributed to banishing "unclean spirits," so it is not surprising that His followers were also known for having this ability. Ridding a person of the demonic has always been considered an important work of Christianity.

With other cultures, there are other beliefs and different methods. Whether they are Voodoo doctors in Africa, Kahunas in Hawaii or Shamans in other parts of the world, there are elaborate rituals to rid a person of evil spirits. Belief in good and bad spirits seems to be worldwide.

Developed over many centuries, the Catholic form of Exorcism has become a lengthy ritual. It is seldom used today because the Church believes there are few true cases of demonic possession. To have the Church declare a person possessed, he or she must perform some preternatural act that could not be accomplished naturally, such as speaking a language not con-sciously known, or having superhuman strength.

From my viewpoint, for these conditions to exist, the demon must be of an extremely high rank and have an ulterior motive for attracting such attention. Usually, they hide them-selves and are not permitted to speak out loud. In the film, *Exorcist I*, which was based on a combination of some actual incidents, it became obvious that it was the priest the Devil really wanted to destroy.

For only after the demon caused excruciating pain to the child he possessed and had terrorized everyone around, did the desperate priest finally groan, "Take me instead."

By admitting defeat in his ability to Exorcise, the priest was consciously giving the devil permission to possess him. Immediately, the child was released and the priest was controlled by the demon and hurtled to his death. The Devil's mission was completed. He disappeared and the child had no subsequent memory of anything that happened.

The Catholic ritual method seems to have been hard on the clergy. In fact, according to my sources, there is little taught about the Devil in most seminaries. Theologians seem to prefer other subjects and feel there is actually little known about the demonic. The Church knows enough from past experiences, however, that she restricts exorcisms to those considered competent and highly trained.

Reports of events that have happened during Exorcisms would frighten anyone. Many years ago, a young priest told me he was present at an Exorcism where the victim's body stiffened and levitated and ashes came spraying out of his mouth. The man remained a priest, but this type of episode could leave a lasting impression and make some consider another career.

Most Charismatics and Christian Fundamentalists have an unwavering belief in the Devil. They attribute evil, and often other unexplainable things as well, to the Powers of Darkness. In some cases, this results in a fear-based religion which can almost be paranoid. The ideal is to have a healthy balance which respects the powers of the demonic, but concentrates on the greater power of God. Those in Spirit Release work are aware that making judgements about others and allowing fear into the heart are two ways of attracting the evil ones.

The lengthy rituals which some groups use can be quite successful in "casting these demons back into hell." However, there seems to be no assurance that they won't come back later. *Spirit Release Therapists* use a method which assures everyone that there will be no return. There are other surprising differences.

The first is that we operate from a position of love and not from a position of fear or adversity. True, it is important to use an authoritative voice when first talking to whatever demon speaks up. There must be absolutely no fear. Anyone working in fear is in the wrong business. Because Light is always stronger than darkness, God does not have to battle for domain. His creations have free will, but He is always in charge.

When we do release work, and pray for help, it ALWAYS comes. This is God's work and He has special, truly powerful Soul Angels. He has appointed to assist us WHEN WE ASK FOR HELP. Some sessions do take a long time, but we always work with love and ALWAYS with Angelic help. In the end, our clients are ALWAYS "cleaned out."

The next difference, and probably a bigger surprise, is that we feel these demons are misguided souls who have been deceived and we want to save them. Yes, save! Help them understand the error of their ways and, with Angelic assistance, have them go back "home," return to God. We certainly don't want to "cast them back to hell" where they can get recycled and come back to possess someone else. With some of the more powerful demons, we are dealing with dangerous forces and need to protect ourselves as well as make sure these evil doers do not return. Ever!

While conducting a *Spirit Releasement*, I address the head demon as "Commander" until I can get his name. (Only higher ranks have names.) When I insist on talking directly to him, he usually remains hidden and sends out one of the "little ones." If the Angels capture this one, the leader really doesn't care. He has others and has no interest in them except that they give him a feeling of power. He is kept in alliance to Satan through fear and this sense of being powerful.

I don't have to talk to a "little one" for long before I figure out he is trying to deceive me. Then, I say, "You're not the Commander! I don't want to talk to you! I want to talk to whoever is in charge! What's the matter? Is he afraid of me? That's it! He's afraid. Okay, Commander, no more tricks. What kind of a coward are you? What do you have to say to me?"

By this kind of taunting, I can usually flush out the head demon. He may come out snarling and shouting. I've heard, "Get out of here!" "You have no business here!" "I'm not talking to you! Go away!" These are the more pleasant and sociable greetings.

Before I start a session, I pray to God, Jesus, the Angels and Guides who assist and those souls from the Light who might be needed. Of course, I always ask Michael the Archangel for protection. When, through various methods, something dark is detected inside a person, I ask that Angels surround it with a net of Light. Eventually I get someone to speak and, after "pleasant-ries" I ask what they know about the Light. "It will destroy us," "It's bad," "It will burn us," are a few of their answers.

It is easy to get them to look at the Light, but getting the Commander to look is more difficult. Usually I try to get his curiosity aroused. In a low, excited voice, I may say, "You are going to see and feel something you haven't known in a long, long time. Take a quick look. I promise, it won't hurt you. What is it you feel?"

It may take a bit of talking to get him over his fear, but eventually, he looks and says, in amazement, "Warm. It feels warm." He is then encouraged to feel how wonderful that is.

From what I gather, hell must be a cold, dark, lonely place where no one can talk. When I hear the voice say, "warm," I'm certain I have a demon. I then explain that making him afraid of the Light was the first way he was deceived. To discover the next way, I have him look deep inside of himself. This can also take some time, but eventually, he will see a small Light inside of himself. Few seem to know what it is, although I've been given such answers as, "My Source," or "Heaven."

I quickly tell him, "That is your spark of God consciousness. Yes, it is IN you. God created you out of love and put His Light in you. You thought you left God, but He has never left you. Your master covered you with all that dark stuff so that you wouldn't know what you truly are. Yes, YOU are a spark of God consciousness. Watch the Light. Is it getting bigger? What's happening to you?"

In total shock, the demon usually replies, "My darkness is fading. The Light is becoming brighter. How can this be?"

By now, my tone softens and warms for most of them. I gently encourage, "Look at the Angels holding the nets of Light, my friend. Look in their eyes and ask them what they want."

After a pause, they may reply: "They want to take me with them; home to the Light. Is this true?"

"Yes, it is. Your master told you that you could never go back. That was another of his deceits. But look! The Angels will take you if you're willing to change. You ARE going to be pulled out of this human. Would you like to go back and tell your master you failed or would you prefer to go with the Angels?"

Given this choice, most stiffen with terror. The thought of going back and admitting failure is the last thing they want to do. Their perception of what will happen to them seems to vary greatly but is always unpleasant. "I'll have my skin peeled off," one said. Considering demons are spirits and don't have bodies, this seemed improbable, but he believed it.

At this point, most happily allow the Angels to pull them out. I want to make sure every last one is out, so I ask, "How many little ones do you have under you?" The answer has ranged from two to hundreds. In the latter situation, I know I will have one confused human to deal with after the releasement.

"Can you get them all out?" I ask the Commander.

"Of course! They do what I tell them. Everyone, get out. Now!"

In some cases, where the Commander is still struggling, the Angels are getting out the "little ones" who are quite happy to leave. With his power base gone, this is another push for the reticent leader. There are several techniques used for the more difficult cases, but in the end, the Angels always win.

A crucial step is next as I instruct the demons, "Look in the Angels' eyes and tell me what you see."

The answer may be "Love," "Peace," "Kindness," etc.

"Excellent. Now tell me, what do you think about what you did to Joe [I say whatever my client's name is]?"

"Oh, it was terrible. I'm really sorry."

"Then, I think you need to tell Joe."

Sometimes this requires a little encouragement as it is quite a new idea. "I'm sorry, Joe," they finally say with true sincerity. The more loquacious ones may even express contriteness for several minutes.

When they finish, I again commend them and start the next step. "Well done. Now, for you to return to Heaven, there is one more thing for you to do. Look into the Angels' eyes again and FEEL the love. When you can feel it, send that love to Joe."

Most are able to do it quickly, but since it is such an unfamiliar feeling for them, some really choke on getting it out.

Finally, they are able to say, "I love you Joe."

If our ex-demon has been easy to work with and is truly sorry for his past, I often say, "I know you are really upset about how you were deceived and what you have done to people. The Angels and I would like you to help others, the way we have helped you. Would you call to all those throughout the Universe, of your rank and below, to come here so you can explain to them how they too have been deceived and how they can now go back to God with the Angels?"

Fear may creep in as they worry about what they could attract. I reassure them that Michael the Archangel's group has a sheer curtain which will not allow any spirits in, but it will allow those outside to see in and hear what is said. With this assurance, they readily agree and begin summoning other dark energy forms. In the meantime, I pray for more Angels to come as guides for those who want to return "home."

Within a short time our Commander reports that other demons are coming. There may be only a few, but usually there are hundreds. With a "general" or other high ranking ex-demon, there can be thousands. "Are they listening to you? Are they going to go with the Angels?" I ask, getting quite excited myself.

"Yes to both questions," is the answer. "A few are flying away, but most of them are going with the Angels. They are extremely happy and so am I."

This is truly an emotional moment for everyone as we realize the thousands who have been saved on this significant day. At the end, I say, "Great! You've done magnificent work. Now you may go to the Light with our love and blessings. Good-bye. And thank you, Angels, for doing this wonderful work."

In any religion, conveying sorrow for one's deeds and sincerely expressing love while wishing to return to God, is salvation. *Spirit Releasers*, or *Soul Workers*, feel the result of their efforts is salvation of the highest order. Most of us were brought up to believe that the demons were eternally damned. It is with great joy that we find it is not so. Also, we know that our clients will have a great lightening of spirit and a much easier life after their release.

Realizing the devils are other creations of a loving God, spiritual creations which have souls to be saved, is a quantum leap of understanding. Our sweet *Soul Worker*, Harmony, once asked, "Couldn't we call them severely unenlightened Angels? I don't like to call them devils."

Therapists haven't worried about becoming politically correct with the demonic. Our clients are our main concern. Perhaps we'll need to think about it some day. In the meantime, keeping as many Satanic forces as possible away from the earth is an important goal.

All of the adventures I have had with the demonic would easily fill a book. While I am no longer surprised by some of the more incredible situations, each one is quite different. In the end, however, they are all removed. Hundreds of therapists are now having the same 1and getting the same results. This does require new thinking. The demonic in Heaven? It does seem so although it appears that they are taken to a different place from humans. An Angel rehab? Perhaps.

While mainstream clergy, and most people, try to avoid discussing the Devil, law enforcement is being forced to face it as the only possible explanation for certain happenings. Even the TV show *20/20* did a documentary on Satanism and gang relationships and also its occurrence in the prison system.

Don, a Hypnotherapist, was with the Wisconsin Department of Corrections for 21 years. I met him at Dr. Baldwin's Intermediate Spirit Release class in California. Don said he belongs to the Midwest Gang Investigation Association in Wisconsin. Much of what the members see seems to be plain dysfunctional gang behavior, but they are also seeing Satanic ritual crimes. These are easily spotted by those familiar with the rituals for they follow a distinct pattern.

Don says his group exchanges information with other Associations throughout the country. They all are becoming acutely aware of grisly crimes that show ritual signs. The offenders have no material gain in mind when there is sexual abuse or animal and human dismemberment.

Dr. Baldwin claims that thousands are killed each year in these rituals. Some female members of these groups, known as "breeders," are forced to produce babies which they must give up to be killed and dismembered in a ritualistic ceremony. The sacrificial victim's remains are cremated so no clue is ever found.

When Havenwyck Psychiatric Hospital in Auburn Hills, Michigan, sponsored a seminar on Satanism, there was standing room only. The Oakland Press, a Michigan daily newspaper, ran a front-page headline reading, "We Ignore Signs of Satanism, Experts Say."[1] Attendees included area psychologists, police officers, mental health experts and school officials. The newspaper article quoted Birmingham psychologist, Linda Green, as saying, "Satanism is all around us, but people would rather turn a blind eye than face the awful truth."

Another speaker, Dale W. Griffis, an expert on mind control and cults, told the audience that he knew of situations where students were dropping heavy hints on teachers and counselors that they had violent tendencies, but the signals were ignored until after a tragedy occurred. "There are second graders drawing pictures of cats cut up and demonic figures," he said. "These children need help, but there is such a tendency toward disbelief that nothing is done."

According to another speaker Dr. Larry E. Dumont, a child and adolescent psychologist many family units have deteriorated so badly that the children no longer have a sense of a secure home. He said that the thinking was twisted, but children and adolescents are turning to violent cures which offer them some of the support they are missing at home.

The newspaper article quoted Dr. Dumont as saying, "We'd like to think of Satan as the Pied Piper playing heavy metal music and leading our children astray. But after we're done, with all the mixed signals we're sending [our children], Satan doesn't have much work left to do."

The doctor said there are many "cults," but the danger comes from the fringe cults which are controlling minds and leading youngsters to crime. He said there are three stages of Satanism: the experimenter playing with a Ouija board; the Satanic dabbler who is getting more seriously involved in the unknown; and the true believer, who has taken Satanism as a religion.

While Hypnotherapists were never mentioned in the article, it is an area they would be most qualified to help with if they have Spirit Release training. Even children can be helped if they are willing. The methods are slightly different, but still the hypnotist talks to attached spirits, human and demonic, and gets them out.

Clients are only told a few things about the process. This way the therapist knows whom he is talking to because clients, attachments and demonic are consistent in responding in different ways. Disbelief on the part of new therapists is common until they see the process and results repeated each time.

Psychiatrist Lawrence Pazder, an M.D. from Canada's British Columbia, was certainly in disbelief for many sessions as he saw his patient, Michelle, regress to childhood and agonize through past memories. Eventually, they collaborated on writing *Michelle Remembers*.[2]

Gory and unforgettable, the book details fourteen months of Michelle's childhood when she was about five and was the "featured attraction" at Satanic rituals. Although the leaders had taken away the child's memories at the end of their dealings with her, she was left with some deep horror inside.

She had seen Dr. Pazder for what she considered minor problems and he was acquainted with her well enough to know she was not the hysterical type. So, he realized something was seriously amiss when she couldn't bring out what was deeply troubling her. One time, desperately squeezing the doctor's hand, she began crying, "There's something I want to tell you, but I don't know what it is. It's important! I know it's important, but I feel blocked."

Putting her into a hypnotic state, Dr. Pazder regressed Michelle back into her early childhood. The horror she began experiencing was so draining that it was necessary to have only a short session. After that day, he hypnotized her many times. With a look of frozen terror, there was a time when she screamed for twenty-five minutes before gasping, "It's all black. Black! No! Oh, please help me. I feel so sick. He's hurting me all over and his eyes are scaring me.

"I don't understand — there are people standing there! They are *laughing*! It isn't funny! Oh, I feel so sick."[3]

For long periods of time the child was left naked in a cage until the cult had a session. Then they would throw her about and rub some foul-smelling substance on her body and even into her eyes, ears and nose.

During some of these seemingly endless rituals, cultists would insert sticks into the rectum of the terrified, naked child while chanting some strange language. When the pain seemed impossible to bear, Mother Mary appeared to Michelle and held her. She then became oblivious to what was going on. This happened on several occasions.

After a time, the cult threw her out for insubordination and she returned home with her mother. With her memories blocked, she appeared to have had a fairly normal childhood after this.

Michelle's mother, an emotionally passive and distant person, had allowed herself to be drawn into the Satanic cult and was forced to give up her little girl to the demands of the group. The child's father, who had been alcoholic and violent, left the family while Michelle was still a baby. Her mother died when she was fourteen and never told her about the rituals.

While Michelle was still captive, Satan himself eventually appeared before the group. It seems he came every seven years. It was in this seventh year of her later years that Michelle would break out in a rash and experience an interior terror she could not understand. At the time she saw Dr. Pazder, it had been twenty-one years since her enslavement to the cult.

Michelle and her doctor decided to make her story known in order to help people understand the evil that exists and what can happen when people get lured into devil worship. It should also assist therapists in realizing the work which might be needed to unlock clients' memories in order to help them finally be rid of terror and panic attacks.

Kids often do crazy things, but what kind of adults are into this bizarre ritualistic behavior? Almost anyone, according to Roxanne, whose father was mayor of their town AND the one responsible for procuring the children for Satanic "sessions."

Roxanne (not her real name) is a beautiful, middle-aged woman with loving, sparkling eyes. She was also at the Intermediate Spirit Release Class where Dr. Baldwin, his wife Judith and members of the class sat spellbound as Roxanne told her shocking history. This was the first time she had publicly told her story and she felt that doing it was part of her own therapy. No one in attendance will ever forget it.

Now an educator, nurse and *Spirit Release Therapist*, Roxanne underwent weekly hypnosis sessions for herself for fourteen years. Considering her gruesome childhood, she was a shining example of what could be done over time with the help of loving, caring therapists.

To all appearances, Roxanne's parents had been truly "proper" people. Yet her father was the leader of a cult and many of his "associates" at these meetings were other town officials or professional people. Roxanne didn't explain how her father got into Satanism, but her aunt was a witch in the group and it seems to have been a "family affair."

It was only after several years of hypnotherapy that Roxanne had a clear picture of what happened to her as a child. Under hypnosis, subjects can remember back to the time when they were in the womb. The remembrance of the events at birth are usually quite clear. So, it is not surprising that Roxanne was able to remember her earliest sexual encounter at eight months when her father brought her to the barn where cult meetings were held. "She's too little," the other men said.

"No, she's not," her father replied and proved his point by penetrating her. It seems the others didn't follow suit until she was three. At that time, Roxanne's mother dressed her up in a fancy dress and told her she was going with her father "to serve." The little girl didn't understand what that meant and so her mother said, "Well, you know how when people come over, we always serve them things to be polite."

Roxanne was taken to the barn and found herself in the middle of a Satanic ritual. She remembers being in a magnificent room with expensive, polished wood and linens. They put the three-year-old in a special chair on a large table and put her legs in stirrups. A belt of some kind was strapped across her to hold her down. They gave her something to drink which may have been a drug. "I was considered the privileged one," she recalled. "Everyone was wearing dark robes and circled around chanting. Then the males all had a turn at sexual intercourse. The pain was excruciating and I took off. Mentally, I was in another place."

(Note: It has been found that often during severe trauma, when children "take off," that other spirits enter and they, eventually, can have Multiple Personality Disorder.)

Roxanne said the ritual took place during a full moon. There was a special room in the barn and three animals were lined up on each side. There was a fire outside and torches inside.

She continued her story: "After I was released, I had incredible stomach aches. The pediatrician, who was probably a cult member, said I had rheumatic fever and needed bed rest. I was in bed from October until June and then had to be taught how to walk again.

"I had a younger brother who was also a Satanic victim. He was in a foster home and my father came and paid some money for him. He had seen the man come before and take other children and they never returned. He was justly terrified. He too had a horrible childhood.

"I was spanked every day by my mother. She said this showed that I was getting enough attention."

By the time she was twelve, Roxanne was too strong to be forced into the barn and, for her, the rituals stopped. She went away to college and eventually married a doctor. For a while, they lived in Europe which was as far away as she could get from her parents.

While they were abroad, she enrolled her children in a preschool and was horrified to find that some of those working there belonged to a Satanic group. It seems that wherever she went, there was always someone trying to get her into a cult.

The most incredible part of her story (which was only briefly told), is that she is still in contact with her parents and visits them at Christmastime. They still try to control her, unsuccessfully, even though she lives in another state.

In answer to astounded classmates, who could not comprehend her maintaining a parental relationship, Roxanne replied, "I feel I'm still working through many things and all the healing I can get before my father dies will help me. Until I have completely forgiven, I cannot be totally healed."

Roxanne's loving countenance attests to her strong spiritual faith and her determination to continue growing. She is involved with working with children and aiding others in seeing the "Light." She is also a sign to those who know her story that anyone can be rescued if they are willing to work at understanding themselves. It can be most painful, but truly rewarding results happen.

Roxanne's present therapist, who was also at the classes, said, "Don't let this scare you. These rituals have power only if you let them. I'm just a guide for Roxanne who really leads every session. At times she feels frightened, but she is brave and determined because many are involved in this Satanic stuff and they need our help. We need to use *Spirit Releasement* on the victims as well as on those who do the evil.

"We need to help people build positive images. If we find someone who has been sexually molested, we shouldn't say, 'poor dear.' This will add to the pain of feeling a victim. Say something like, 'You look beautiful. You survived it and are continuing on. How great.' Help them to get on with their lives with a knowledge of their inner strength. There is a vast difference between being a survivor and being a victim. Roxanne is a beautiful example of someone who trusts in God and is growing and developing. She is already assisting many."

A surprising number of today's senseless crimes can be attributed to possession. Crime has always existed, but because of drugs, alcohol, TV violence and a breakdown of family values, more and more young people are caught in the web of possession. "America faces 'Ticking Crime Bomb' in growing youth" headlined a recent Scripps Howard article about the exploding number of killings by American teenagers.[4]

The article states, "The coming explosion is predicted by projecting the pattern of criminal behavior of today's teenagers onto the next wave of children, those who will reach their mid-teens soon after the year 2,000.

"The number of homicides by teenagers between 14 and 17 has nearly tripled between 1985 and 1995. Increasingly, homicides are impulsive rather than plotted."

Some people seem to have an inner voice urging them to violence or killing. This was true of John Lennon's killer, Mark David Chapman. He was interviewed in Attica State Prison (New York) on the tenth anniversary of Lennon's death by Jack

Jones of Gannett News Service.[5]

Jones writes that Chapman was imagining Lennon's death while 6,000 miles away in Honolulu, "trapped in a disintegrating, demon-ravaged mind." He went to New York and waited for the unsuspecting couple outside their exclusive apartments. "Chapman heard the evil whisperings of a small voice within: 'Do it! Do it! Do it!'"

"And I turned and did it," Chapman said.

"...when the .38 special at last stopped throbbing in his hands, Chapman found himself unable to loosen his fingers from the gun." He couldn't believe what he had done and he prayed that God would turn back time. He has prayed almost every day since then for God's and Lennon's forgiveness.

Jones wrote: "'There's a light moving through every darkness,' Chapman said, describing his search for answers and absolution. 'The idea is to follow in the center of the light as much as you possibly can.'"

For the Spirit Release Therapist, the article gave many clues to demonic possession even before mentioning "an emotionally deprived childhood and drug-hazed adolescence." Not surprisingly, Chapman had had mental problems and had made a serious suicide attempt shortly before the killing.

Following the crime, he could not move or let go of the gun. There was no way his demons would let him avoid getting caught. Back in his own mind, he could not believe what he had done. "Before this, I was basically a decent person," he said.

A demon's job is to get his assigned person to self-destruct in one way or another. I asked one demon, who was speaking through the voice of my client, what would happen if he did convince the person to kill himself. He was completely casual as he replied, "I would leave and go to someone else."

Could Chapman have been prevented from killing if the

therapist who prescribed anti-depressant drugs in Hawaii understood spirit possession? A depossession could easily have been done in two or three hours. It isn't that difficult, once the procedures are learned. This is not to say that other counseling wouldn't be helpful, but only that possession, which isn't that uncommon, needs to be considered first.

A Midwest physician who does Spirit Release work showed a group of therapists drawings made by a 14-year-old boy. Daggers, blood drops, crazy-looking people and demonic signs were sketched on the paper in random fashion, The drawings shouted that here was someone who was one step from major violence.

"He's already in constant trouble, but he's coming around," the doctor said. "When I first saw him, he was so light-sensitive he couldn't remove his dark glasses. Now that we've had some release sessions, he doesn't have to wear the glasses. The 'Light of God' even affects the physical. We've got a lot more work to do, but he is starting to co-operate and there is hope."

On the rare occasion when there is a dealing with a High Demonic, one of the "Generals" of Satan, the protocol is most reserved. You do not ask questions and give instructions in the same way as you would with those of lesser rank. You have prayed and protected yourself with a capsule of God's Light and asked the Holy Spirit to speak for you and not let your ego get in the way. You don't want to think YOU can win an argument. However, I've found that my words seem to flow out and even the Generals are eventually convinced that they have been deceived and that there is a better place for them.

Dr. Baldwin reports that Satan himself does come around now and then to see what is happening. He has lost a lot of troops since depossession work started. "When he arrives, you are most aware that you are in the presence of a powerful being," said the

Doctor.

"You do not have much discussion with him. I did, however, once have the courage to ask him if he was going to the Light. He shocked us by replying, 'Not yet.' This gave us the feeling that he was aware that one day everyone would go back to God."

Dr. Baldwin has written, "Denial and defiance of our spiritual heritage is a denial and defiance of God. At the innermost core, each being knows the truth of its identity. This cannot be denied. It is the way home… every spark of God will return, and eventually all will join in the Oneness. This includes Lucifer, the prodigal son, and his legions of demons."[6]

Listening to Dr. Baldwin do Spirit Release work in his deep, melodic voice which flows in a steady, articulate path, students wonder if they can duplicate his process.

His answer is, "Yes, my work is original, but much of it has evolved from information received while working with clients. I have had many years of practice and the words just come to me. There are always variations on the theme, but those who learn basic skills can trust in the process.

"I'm not gifted, but I am in my flow doing this work. I become absolutely absorbed. I feel the work is important. A lot of what happens comes from just having faith. Of course, it is most helpful to be working with other Spirit Releasers so you can be part of a team and develop a sense of support and community."

Through the dedication of Dr. Baldwin and his wife Judith, hundreds have now taken his course. Many of his students, such as myself, are teaching the information to many more. Others, throughout the world, are learning from his detailed 456-page book, *Spirit Releasement Therapy: A Technique Manual.*

CHAPTER 4

Nature Spirits
Collaborate With Humans

Every visible thing in the world
is under the charge of an Angel.
– ST. AUGUSTINE

$\mathcal{S}$*everal years ago books and* articles about the Findhorn Garden seemed to pop up everywhere I went. Walking down an aisle in the crowded Mayflower bookstore in Berkley, Michigan, a Findhorn book flashed its cover at me like a fire cracker in a dark closet. I could see nothing else. Long ago I learned that when something comes up three or more times in a brief period, I'm supposed to pay attention. "Pay attention!" my Guardian Angel seems to be insisting.

So, I bought the book, read it and, of course, missed the messages completely. I have long suffering Angels and Guides, but fortunately, they never give up on me.

Flowers thrill me and I have had small gardens. But I didn't know what could be important about this strange Garden in a cold northeast Scotland seashore town where they grew forty-pound cabbages, eight-foot delphiniums and had roses blooming in the snow? Nice, but only of passing interest like the nearby Loch Ness monster.

The story is that in late 1962 Peter Caddy lost a prestigious job and, with his family of six, was forced to live in a small trailer in Findhorn Bay Caravan Park. Jobs eluded him, but the family had strong spiritual training and gave their lives over to God (the first point I wasn't supposed to miss). Caddy's wife, Eileen, and their friend Dorothy Maclean, were both clairaudient. That is, they heard spiritual voices. When they were first told to start a garden, it seemed totally illogical. They were living in a sandy area with some gravel and wild shrubs.

The voices, from Nature Spirits, were quite definite about how they were to prepare the soil. Since they lived on a small unemployment check, they had no money for supplies. No problem. Whatever they needed was always provided whether it was manure, straw, potash, seed or other material. The women remained in contact with Nature Spirits, sometimes called devas, and Peter worked mightily in the garden and followed his strong intuitions.

The group was also told that they must work with love and learn to cooperate with the devas and elementals who were experimenting with assisting humans. The first summer they had a successful garden and were able to sell some of the extra vegetables.

What was happening? During meditation, Peter realized they were pioneering something new. He wrote: "For the first time, Western man is consciously working, hand-in-hand, with the spiritual aspects of the nature kingdoms." That evening Eileen heard this Angelic message: "Tell Peter that what illuminated him this morning was indeed so. You are working with nature, with the devas and elementals, and are gradually finding harmony with them. What is now happening is something new, and this is the way the world is to be recreated."

"All we had was ourselves, our positive thoughts and faith in God's unlimited abundance. In learning to see the world in terms of causes rather than effects, we had to rely on God as the source of all supply rather than looking to a salary and bank balance for security. The principles we were working with in this were not new; they are part of the ancient wisdoms, but they have no reality unless they are lived and proved."[1]

This is sometimes called "The Principle of Manifestation."

By the second year, the faith and confidence of the small family had grown. There was much physical work as well as relying on God. Everything was provided and all their needs were met. During 1964 they grew an astonishing sixty-five different types of vegetables, twenty-one kinds of fruits and forty-two different herbs. Each type of plant had its own special deva which was welcomed as seeds were sowed or the plants set out.

The devas and other nature spirits not only outdid themselves with quantity but flavor as well. Word of the Findhorn Garden quickly spread and, eventually, gardening experts arrived. "This is impossible" they grumbled, but soil samples came back showing perfect soil and the results were obviously there. Not willing to admit to Angelic-human collaboration at first, Peter just attributed everything to improving the soil and "Love."

Visitors looked for artificial fertilizers as though it would be impossible for nature alone to produce such miracles. And what did "Love" have to do with it? Absolutely everything.

Eventually, the word was out and Findhorn became a working and spiritual community of about 200. No longer did vegetables need to be gigantic. That detracted from the main focus of showing that humans could now work in co-operation with the Angelic kingdoms. When I first read about Findhorn, I thought that this unity of purpose was only for the land. Wrong! Now I understand that Angels are here to help us in ALL matters that are for the good of mankind.

Eleven years after Findhorn Community was started, American writer, Paul Hawken, visited the Garden and wrote: "Everywhere I put my hand into the soil there was sand two or three inches under the compost. It is like gardening on a beach. Yet staring at you and waving brightly in the sun is a compact bunch of healthy flowers. It defies rational analysis and so far, no scientific authority has been able to explain the phenomenon of Findhorn."[2]

Hawken said that the current gardeners did not see the Nature Spirits, but felt intuitively guided by them in their work. As for Peter Caddy, he was "having fun" as he directed the activities of the fast growing community. He was even joyful as he recounted his failures.

He said that he had made so many mistakes that he couldn't count them. And every one was a Divinely-guided message, something for him to learn.

He told about having a gallstone operation so that the community was forced to function without him and he had to learn to let go. "We are moving into the age of group consciousness, and I had to learn to work with a group, not as an individual," he explained. (Another universal lesson.)

Author Hawken also quoted Caddy as saying, "It's very important that people know the significance of Findhorn. Here we are actually demonstrating God's plan in concrete ways. We are not just talking a lot of airy fairy stuff about His greatness and how you should live in faith. We are embodying it! We are living it! It's most important that people see that this works, that all of man's needs can be met if he is willing to surrender his life to God. We didn't say anything about devas or elves for years. We just kept it to ourselves because we knew people couldn't understand it until it had been demonstrated. Only after years of results, and after experts from around the world confirmed the results, could we say to the world: This is how we did it!"[3]

Slowly, and often painfully, I had learned the "The Laws of Abundance" or "The Laws of Manifestation" as Caddy calls it. Circumstances in my life have been miraculously taken care of so many times that I couldn't begin to count them. If I start to worry about something now, my Angel gets a bit testy and I hear: "How many times do you have to see that it will all turn out right?"

The Findhorn experience may not be commonplace today, but many people will tell you that they talk to their plants. Horticulturist Cindy McGonagle from Portland, Oregon, is almost casual in writing about having a co-creative experience in your own garden when telepathically listening to plant devas. She suggests imagining the spirit of the plant within, touching it and saying, "I love you."

As many others have suggested, she mentions the Angel of the area that oversees the land and lovingly guides the devas and elementals for each group of plants. If a plant or tree has stress, it calls an Angelic equivalent of 9-1-1 and other Nature Spirits are sent to aid its healing.

In *Angel Times*, McGonagle writes: "Plant devas are mature intelligence of pure light energy who hold an exact knowledge of each plant's perfect form no matter what physical changes may happen.

"[By listening] You will be able to get messages quickly about fertilizers, soil and light conditions as you move within the energy field of each plant. Afterwards, always thank the devas for their help...

"Remember each of us has a gift to share with healing the earth. Begin to listen to the messages from the nature kingdom. They help us to recreate Heaven on Earth."[4]

When I asked Angel Samora about devas and/or Angels, rainbows and color, she replied: "Angels and rainbows, we're all of the Light. When light comes into your universe, it changes, like through a prism. It is the job of some Angels to help it come through and change into the vibrations of different colors. So, you have an Angel who works with the blue, one with the green, one with the purple and so on. Each color has a specific thing it does for your body, such as helping the heart and the emotions.

"Understand, it is through your feeling nature, through the heart, that all things manifest. It is this portal that is the most important for the emotions hold the spiritual and they cannot come into your heart unless you allow them. Your soul is you. It is throughout you, although the emotions that affect your soul may come through the heart portal."

I asked, "What about the plant devas and other Nature Spirits? Some seem to actually see them. In Ireland, it seems general knowledge that there are 'Little people.' Is this so?"

Samora answered: "Some do see them. They were raised to believe in their existence and it opens their senses up to see. Everyone in your country has been taught that "Little people" are just a superstitious belief. In places where they don't believe it is superstition, their eyes are open and it is natural and normal for many to see them. Your *Soul Worker*, Harmony, sees them."

"Really?" I asked in surprise. "She has never said anything about seeing them. Of course, I'm not surprised. She is so clairvoyant that she sees many things that the rest of us don't."

She has a clan of gnomes and fairies who live by her house

that she sees all the time. She loves them and they consider her one of their protectors, Samora informed me.

While some see or hear Nature Spirits, they are rarely written about in much detail. That is why the books by Geoffrey Hodson from England are such classics. In *The Brotherhood of Angels and Men* Hodson writes:

> *The ideal of this brotherhood is to draw angels and men, two branches of the infinite family of God into close co-operation in order to uplift the human race.*
>
> *To this end the angels, on their side, are ready to participate as closely as possible in every aspect of human life and in every human activity where co-operation is possible.*
>
> *Those humans who will throw open heart and mind to their brethren of the other sphere, will find an immediate response, and a gradually increasing conviction of its reality.*[5]

In another of his books, Fairies *at Work and at Play*, Hodson describes so many different spirits that he has seen that it boggles the mind of those of us who don't see. He has chapters on Brownies and Elves, Gnomes, Mannikins, Undines and Sea Spirits, Fairies, Sylphs, Devas and Elementaries.

Most of these spirits are then divided again so that there are wide divergencies within each type. For instance, Tree Gnomes are larger than the others at about two feet, six inches high.

Rock Gnomes appeared not quite evolved and manifest in rock as formless blotches of color which make the rock seem transparent. A Domestic Gnome peers into people's houses and then tries to imitate them in dress and manner. Hodson saw one descend into the earth two or three feet and move about without obstruction. It appeared he thought that was his home.

The Dancing Gnomes are only four to six inches high and love to play in groups. They are gaily colored and seem to have little intelligence as they dance and go through antics. And, finally, there are the Moorland Gnomes who appear to be male and about two feet high. Their mouths are set in a perpetual grin and they can travel through the air with great speed if they wish. Hodson gives many other details about these spirits whom he observed at various times.

Hodson was obviously entranced by the seldom seen but fascinating Undine, a water spirit which is always found in a river, stream or waterfall. Her diminutive female form is usually seen without wings or adornment. He writes:

> *The waterfall is her favorite haunt, and there she is to be seen disporting herself, generally with a group of her sisters, enjoying to the full the magnetic force of the fall.*
>
> *Poised amid the spray, or in the center of the downward rushing torrent, she absorbs, slowly, the magnetism from the sunlight and the waterfall; as the limit of absorption is reached, she releases, in one dazzling flash of light and color, the energy with which she is surcharged. At that magical moment of release, she experiences an ecstasy and exaltation beyond anything possible to mere mortals dwelling in the prison of the flesh. The eyes flash with dazzling radiance and the face expresses rapturous joy which altogether produces a vision of enchanting loveliness.[6]*

Hodson believes that there are probably many other kinds of water spirits. The possibilities of what exists in our unseen world seem to be endless.

A delightful, modern American lady, Molly Sheehan of Meriden, New Hampshire, has animated conversations with Angels, devas and a host of other spirits. She lives on Green

Hope Farm with her husband, four children, three cats, one dog and seventeen chickens.

Her cooperative adventure with the spirit world began in 1988 with a conversation in the asparagus bed. It was late spring and she wondered why there was no asparagus poking up. "We are coming," she heard a deep voice say in her mind. She assumed her mind was playing tricks and shook her head to refocus. But the words continued, "Actually, it's been a cold spring so we are taking our time. But more importantly, we really do not like this location and would like you to move us. Right behind the roses would be nice."

MOVE an asparagus patch? That was definitely not her idea. While she stood wide-eyed, another voice was heard. "And while you're moving things, it would be a good idea to take your raised beds apart. They do not work."

In a newsletter, Molly wrote, "Ever since I read about the Findhorn Gardens where people conversed with plants, I had hoped and prayed to hear from mine. I just hadn't considered what they would say.

"With a shovel at my side, I have been talking with Nature ever since. The Angels, who hold the Divine blueprint for the farm, guide me in designing gardens which are in alignment with God's plan for the farm. Their very specific directions have led to the creation of gardens of unusual geometry, high vibrations, great abundance and beauty.

The elementals, including the fairies and gnomes, are equally important to our efforts here. They are responsible for manifesting all ideas into actual physical form and so are essential for transforming the Angelic designs into vibrant herbs, flowers and vegetables. In addition, they have learning lessons for me, the Human gardener.

From the beginning I was guided to make Flower Essences. These beautiful vibrational remedies work on our electrical systems to rebalance our emotional, spiritual, mental and physical selves when we are out of balance in any way. I am awed by the Divine wisdom and healing energy available to us in Flower Essences. I feel very blessed that Green Hope Farm's mission is to bring the Flower's gifts to Humankind.[7]

After eight years of talking to the spirit world, Molly is quite knowledgeable about whom she is talking to and is particularly spirited in her replies. She is quite capable of letting them know what they MUST do or what she MUST have.

In her newsletters and in her speeches to audiences, she talks as though everyone knows about Angels, devas, elementals and other Nature Spirits and constantly converses with them. Her own zany conversations with them often make highly amusing stories. For instance, one time she was giving orders to whomever was in charge of the ants crawling into her house. They were to get them out! She would be back in fifteen minutes to see that they were gone. When she came back, most were gone and she was assured that the few stragglers would soon leave.

I became familiar with Flower Essences in 1980 with the Bach Flower Remedies which were the first to be developed in this century. Edward Bach was a medical doctor in England who loved mankind and all of nature. An open-minded forward thinker, he discovered a medical connection between feelings and actual physical illness. He believed that the disharmonies and fears of the heart and the spirit must be the focus of a healer's attention.

Abandoning traditional medicine in 1930, he scoured the

hillsides and eventually found thirty-eight non-poisonous plants and trees which could put emotions into a better balance. Using only the flowers, he prepared his remedies using Homeopathic methods. Anywhere from four to six different remedies are selected for a person's "Formula" and poured into a one-ounce dropper bottle. Four drops are taken four times a day in water or juice. Over sixty years of dramatic results have convinced millions of the efficacy of Flower Remedies.

No one knows if Dr. Bach actually talked to Nature Spirits, but he was so highly intuitive and spiritual that he was obviously inspired by a Higher Voice of some kind.

In *Heal Thyself*, Dr. Bach wrote: "Behind all disease lies our fears, our anxieties, our greed, our likes and dislikes. Let us seek those out and heal them, and with the healing will go the disease from which we suffer."

He also wrote: "Bodily ills are only symptoms. The Flower Remedies do not attack disease, but like beautiful music, flood our natures with the virtues we need. As our Higher Natures prevail, disease melts as snow in the sunshine."[8]

Since the Remedies feed our Spiritual Natures, they do not interfere with any other healing methods, not even medicines. They are also quite compatible with wholesome food and food supplements. RESCUE, a combination of five Remedies, is the most famous of Bach's formulas and is used for emergencies, traumas, phobias and severe stress such as stage fright.

When I first took the Bach Flower Remedy course in 1980, my skeptical nature made it difficult for me to accept such amazing results from some "watered down flowers." What was worse, our instructor said that we would "instinctively know" which Remedies to use for ourselves and our clients.

Yes, there were times when I just "knew" things, but my

faith in intuition was slight and I was nowhere near the time when I would talk to Angels and Guides.

I received encouragement, however, from G. Khalsa, a Medical Doctor in our class who said, "I'm already using the Remedies on some of my patients. They work subtly but very deeply. You will be surprised at how much they help people."

Well, I *was so surprised* that after a few years I began to teach classes on Bach Flower Remedies. My students were having so much trouble remembering the thirty-eight different Remedies, however, that in 1991 I wrote a book, *How To Remember Bach Flower Remedies or… First, Get The Elephant Off Your Foot.*[9] It contains a humorous cartoon for each Remedy and details what it is used for and what the results are.

I still wasn't working with Angels, but in retrospect, I can see that many of my efforts were inspired. The Angels were already leading me to make sure that their efforts toward getting humans to collaborate with Nature would advance.

All this is presented to help you understand that most of us don't suddenly wake up and start having exciting conversations with our Angels and Guides. Nor do we immediately have complete confidence in them. Some may, but most humans have to start with a desire for this co-operation as Molly Sheehan had. It takes time.

When someone asked Molly how they could start talking with their Angel, she replied, "I believe that Angels and others from the spirit world first talk to us across the bridge of our imagination. This is often how we visited together as children. In rekindling the imagination, we re-ignite the connection. Just imagine you are having a conversation with your beloved Angel guides and then listen to what you hear and see what you can. Try to do so without clouding the picture with editorial judgments. Trust in the process. It will take you across the bridge into open communication with God and all God's creations."[10]

In addition to Molly's excellent suggestions, I know that your Angel wants to communicate with you AT LEAST as much as you want to talk with her. Also, be aware that children OFTEN see their Angels and their "imaginary friends" might actually be real.

It was through my interest in Flower Remedies that I eventually learned about Molly's work on Green Hope Farm. I was particularly intrigued by her "sources of information" in the spirit world. I had begun talking with Angels by then, but never connected them with the Flower Essences I had been preparing for twelve years. (As I said, I have really patient Angels.)

I was thrilled when Molly began preserving her Remedies with Red Shiso, an organically-grown herb. Bach and other Flower Essences prepared throughout the world have always been stabilized with brandy. Many are opposed to this, especially if they are in an Addiction-Free program.

I was amazed, and somewhat overwhelmed, by the more than 100 flowers Molly had potentized for all the new energies on earth. For instance, there is Petunia St. Germain for forgiveness and transmutation of all negativity; Angelica which knits wounds in physical, mental, emotional and spiritual bodies; Water Hyacinth which teaches nonjudgment and balance in all our emotional experiences. It helps us see essential gifts in all emotion.

Molly has also formulated Essences for animals, for addictions and for emergency care (somewhat different from Rescue). Then, there is Date Palm which rejuvenates the entire system and encourages the distribution of Life Force energy to every cell in the body. All of Molly's remedies have been the result of Angel-Human collaboration.

Accepting results from such efforts is difficult for our left-brained world, but there is scientific evidence available. Before Molly started her work, Rev. Franklin Loehr was experimenting with plants and eventually wrote, *The Power of Prayer on Plants*.[11] Coming from a scientific as well as a spiritual background, Rev. Loehr made every effort to conduct valid research. He enlisted 156 volunteers to perform 700 experiments, with 100,000 measurements on 27,000 seeds. Not a small undertaking.

Many different controlled experiments were conducted. Plants and/or seeds were divided into three groups with each group receiving a different treatment. One group was talked to and prayed for; another group was talked to negatively and the third group was just watered with no talking or prayer. Nearly always, the group that was prayed for, did better. In some cases there was as much as 52.71% improvement in the growth and the health of the plants.

Following this, Peter Tompkins and Christopher Bird's book, *Secret Life of Plants*, was published in 1973 and it became a best seller. Extensive research was done in Europe and the Soviet Union as well as the United States to show that plants have emotions, and some can read minds, diagnose disease and a host of other astonishing abilities.

The authors claim that Viennese biologist Raoul France could have written a similar book at the beginning of the century, but he shocked "vegetal scientists" by suggesting that the awareness of plants might originate in a supra-material world. How heretical in those days to suggest there were devas and other spirits involved in plants! Today "there are skeptics who find it hard to believe that plants may at last be the bridesmaids at a marriage of physics and metaphysics,"[12] say the authors.

Tompkins' and Bird's experiments got many thinking with

the result that many more people began to converse with their plants if not with devas.

The progression of modern experiments from plants to humans took time, but when they were scientifically conducted, the results were the same. Prayer works! Double-blind studies were actually done in a hospital on sick people. Some were prayed for, some weren't, and some received both prayer and therapy.

Larry Dossey, a traditional medical doctor who originally believed prayer was a superstition, was stunned to discover scientific evidence of the healing power of prayer. He now lectures internationally and his *Healing Words*[13] book is a must for those who wish further evidence that linking prayer, healing and medicine is a giant step forward in integrating science and spirituality.

While I did not hear him talk about Healing Angels when I attended one of his lectures, I think that may come someday. Angels are exceedingly persistent.

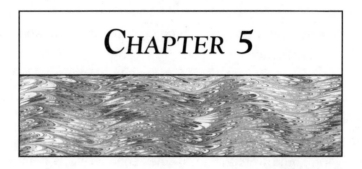

CHAPTER 5

The "Student" Appears

$\mathcal{N}$ot all of The Soul Workers came as students. There was the unusual case of Balbir who first came as a client. It started when a local medical doctor had his receptionist call and quiz me about Spirit Release work. I explained briefly since I didn't know this doctor or how he found out about me. (After all, I didn't need any problems from the medical establishment.) Then, she really surprised me by asking, "Do you work with a medium?"

Oh, dear! How to answer this? Finally, in my best professional voice, I said, "I have an assistant who seems to have some gifts for knowing about people and sometimes helps me with clients. We don't use the term 'medium.' Why are you asking?"

"The doctor may have someone to send to you. Do you and the medium have any time tomorrow?"

I wished she would stop calling Kathy a "medium," but I cooly responded, "If my assistant is available, we could see someone tomorrow afternoon about one o'clock."

"Fine. I'll call you back."

I really didn't expect anything to come of it. I went back

to work, but kept wondering how the doctor knew about me since I do not advertise. About five minutes later, the phone rang and the same voice said, "The doctor's friend would like to have your one o'clock appointment. His name is Balbir and he will be coming with his sister who needs help. How does he get to your office?"

After giving her the directions, I called Kathy who, fortunately, was available. "I don't know what this is all about, but we'll pray that we can help someone," I told her. Then, remembering that her "dress code" was usually blue jeans, I said, "Since these people are coming from a medical doctor, I think we need to dress as professionally as possible."

"No blue jeans?"

"No blue jeans."

She grumbled a little but came early the next day in her best slacks. We then prayed together and set up the recorder. Through the office window, we saw a mini-van pull up. Out stepped a tall, dark gentleman and three women. One of the women was barely able to walk. She was supported by the man as they made their way to the door.

"Hello, I'm Balbir. Dr. Kay made an appointment for my sister." He sort of smiled but looked very upset. We got them all into the large waiting room because my office was too small for six. We were introduced to Melissa, Balbir's wife, and to the older woman who was his mother. His sister, our client, was in such a stupor she couldn't acknowledge us. She was a dental surgeon in India and had come to the U.S. with her mother for a brother's wedding in another city. For some time the sister had been under psychic attack from a very strong spirit entity. She had made the trip from India and gotten through the wedding, but her situation had progressively worsened. The spirit harassed her day and night so that she could not sleep.

In the brother's city, they had taken her to a psychiatrist who prescribed Prozac (which takes two weeks to take effect). She was supposed to return to India in three days, but it would be almost impossible for her to travel in this condition. She had not been able to sleep at all for four days and, in a semi-conscious state, sat on the couch like a limp rag.

Balbir said they expected to have to take her back to India for help. They didn't know anyone in the U.S. knew how to do Spirit Release. They had brought her to their home in Michigan in the hope that his friend, Dr. Kay, could do something for her.

It was obvious that Balbir didn't want to go into much detail, but he told us that the spirit had attached to his sister while she was working on a dental patient. The family knew the patient and thought he was a special "holy man." However, there was a dark side to him that they had only recently learned about. Could we help?

"We'll do everything we can," I replied. "We have some powerful angels who help us."

I explained a little about our method for getting rid of spirits and they agreed to let us try. With everyone looking on, Kathy got into a comfortable position and I said the Pra*yer for Protection*:

> *The Light of God surrounds us; the love of God enfolds us; the power of God protects us and the presence of God watches over us. Wherever we are, God is and all is in Divine Order.*

Then I added:

> *Father/Mother God, thank you for bringing us together and for helping us. Brother Jesus and Mother Mary, we thank you for coming with your great love and concern. Michael, the Archangel, we ask you to be here to protect us*

*and not let any darkness in. Mighty Warrior Angels, please
assist us. We also ask for those from the Light who might be
needed. We pray that all of our Guardian Angels and Spirit
Guides will be here with us and, also, any others who wish
to help us. If there are any spirits here who have not gone
to the Light, you may listen, but under no circumstances,
may you enter anyone or speak through any of us. If you
wish to go home to the Light when we finish, an Angel will
be happy to take you.*

We add the last part because Angel Athena had once told
us that, when we did our work, we sometimes were helping
nearby spirits who were attracted by the magnificent Light of the
Angels who came. We were totally unaware of them but happy
that some "extras" were getting in. At the same time, we needed
to protect everyone so that these wandering souls didn't attach
or start talking through someone.

After Kathy went into deep relaxation, Athena came
through in about two minutes and greeted us solemnly. We were
dealing with a very ancient and powerful spirit, she told us, and
it was necessary for the Warrior Angels to surround him with a
net of Light immediately. It was vital that he not get away.

As we started talking to Athena, we realized that the
possessed woman was beginning to moan and writhe around as
if in pain. The family looked on in fright and became more and
more uncomfortable. This wasn't going to be supportive if they
were sending worry vibrations around the room. "Athena," I
commented, "they are getting nervous. Can we have the spirit
speak through Kathy but not possess her?"

"Yes, she can do that. Give the spirit instructions."

In a stern voice, I said, "All right spirit, we see you are there.
You have gotten that poor woman so exhausted, you can't speak

through her. However, see the one lying quietly here? You may not... repeat NOT... possess her in any way, but you may speak through her. What do you want to say?"

Almost at once, the sister went limp and quiet, but the lovely face of Kathy became distorted with rage. From her mouth came an angry snarl. "How dare you do this!" a male voice demanded. "Get out of here! She's mine!" By now he was shouting. "You can't do anything, you silly woman. I'm too powerful! Get away!"

In a low, confident voice, I answered. "You may have some power, evil one, but there are strong Angels here who are much more powerful than you. We don't have to shout because there is a strong net of Light around you that came from God. Feel it and you will see."

"I don't want to feel it," he shrieked in frustration. "You take it away! I must have her. She's mine, I tell you. GO AWAY!"

"We are NOT going away! She is not yours! You can feel the Light peacefully or you can feel the net getting tighter and tighter around you. Soon you won't be able to breathe. Look at the Light! You will see and feel something you haven't felt in a long, long time."

"NO!" he cried but more from terror than with force.

"Go ahead. Take a look." I taunted him, "Of course, a big powerful one like you wouldn't be afraid to look, would you? Ha! That's it. You're afraid."

"Am not," he sneered. "See." Kathy's head snapped quickly to one side and then back.

"Well, that wasn't long enough to see or feel anything," I chided. "Besides, notice that the Light didn't destroy you. What is it that's there that you're not suppose to know about?"

Kathy's head moved cautiously to one side and then back. After a short pause, the entity turned back for a longer look.

"Well, are you seeing something, sir?" I asked. "Tell us. What is it that you've seen?"

"Peace. I feel peace. I'd forgotten what it was like. I've been in this evil state for centuries. I just don't..." his voice trailed off in confusion.

When he said "centuries," I realized that I was dealing with a spirit that had once been a human since the demonic do not know time. I ventured an educated guess. "You were once a human, but you wanted more power. You sold yourself to the devil. Were you a warlock?"

"Yes," he said in a soft voice. "I was VERY powerful. I could even control the elements. Many were afraid of me and did anything I asked." Some of the braggadocio began to come out again.

"Well, you don't have much power right now. Those Angels aren't going to let you get away. Your arrogance has caught up with you. So, you agreed to work for the devil. Has he kept any of his promises to you in the last couple of hundred years?"

"No. [Pause.] Not one of them."

"Well, he deceived you into doing his dirty work." I whispered in my best attorney-like voice, "If he didn't do what he said, that's breach of contract. You can get out of this deal."

A look of sheer terror came over Kathy's face and the evil one nearly choked as he cried, "I couldn't. He would... oh, he'd do terrible things to me."

"No! He CANNOT get into the Light," I assured him. "Look into the eyes of the Angels who are holding the net. What do you see? Ask them what they want of you."

"I see... love. It's pure love. Oh! My! They want to take me 'home'... to the Light. Ohhh, could I really go?"

"Well, that's up to you. You've done some pretty awful things to people. Keep looking into the eyes of the Angels and tell me how you feel about what you've done," I instructed.

"Oh, terrible. It was so bad. I just wanted power. I had no idea what would happen. I'm really sorry."

As the spirit continued talking, I discovered that his job was to help stop Balbir's family from some powerful spiritual work that they were supposed to do which would help many. Demonic forces wanted to stop them by making their lives unbearable. The former warlock showed great remorse and soon I was able to get him to apologize to the sister and actually send love to her. After this, he let the Angels gently lift him out of her body and take him to the Light.

As he lifted off, the sister leaned against her mother and fell into a deep sleep. Her exhausted body became totally relaxed and her breathing was normal. The family looked on in amazement.

Athena then spoke through Kathy. "He is gone and won't return. He is sorry for his misdeeds, so he can be rehabilitated. He will be taken to a place where he can rest for a while and then he will go to the Halls of Learning. He is highly intelligent even though he was misguided. He'll learn quickly. Now you may finish the work."

I prayed for what we call the "Clean-up Team" to come and clean out any residue from the attachments. Then, I asked the Angels to come and fill the sister's sleeping body with Healing Light. While this was happening, I stood and smoothed out her aura, her magnetic field, by passing my hands about four or five inches around and over her body. A sense of peace came over the woman's face as she continued her deep sleep.

When I was finished, I asked Kathy to open her eyes, be wide awake, alert and feeling great. When she sat up, she exclaimed, "Oh, my! That was really a bad one!"

When she channels, Kathy is quite clairvoyant and can

often tell us many details of what happened. As the family sat spellbound, she told them what she had seen of this vicious spirit and his later conversion. I said nothing until they had talked for a while about how fast and successful the process had been. It had only been about an hour-and-a-half since they arrived.

When they finally became quiet and waited for me to speak, I just looked at Balbir and asked, "The spirit indicated that this is a family problem?"

He squirmed in his chair, then looked down and admitted, "Yes, we know about it. It's a long story, but I didn't want to say anything until my sister was taken care of. I'm stronger than she is, but I'm also being attacked. Do you think you could help me, too?"

"Quite likely. This method is usually effective. Of ourselves, we can do nothing, but with prayer and the aid of some really powerful Angels, miracles happen. We have been most blessed to have these beautiful spirits come whenever we need them.

"I am happy to do what I can for you, but you must be completely honest with me. Obviously, we are dealing with something quite different from our usual work. Let's say a prayer of thanksgiving together and then you and I will go into my office while sister sleeps here on the couch."

In my office, after hearing some of Balbir's story, I decided that it was not necessary to know it all now since it covered many years. I put him into a light hypnotic state and began the Spirit Release process. Several entities were attached, some of them dark energy forms or demons. It took nearly two hours, but it ended as it always does. Everyone was truly happy as the Angels took the spirits to the Light.

When Balbir awakened, he seemed to be greatly relieved. "I knew I was protected, but it was a terrible battle. I'm so glad that it's over," he said.

"Someday, when we have time, I hope to hear your whole story, Balbir. It sounds absolutely fascinating. I got just an inkling from what the spirits who were attached to you told me. But now, I think we should rejoin the others and… Balbir, what's the matter?"

He had stopped smiling and was looking ahead but upward. "Oh, no. It's back! There's a spirit that keeps coming into my upper vision. It doesn't cause any disturbance, but it's a terrible nuisance. I'd hoped it was gone. What can we do?"

He was obviously agitated and I felt confused by what was happening. I knew the Angels had gotten him "cleaned out." What were we dealing with? "Well, thankfully, Kathy is here. Perhaps Athena can shed some light on this. Let's go back into the other room."

Balbir's sister was still asleep on the couch and the other three women were enjoying a get-acquainted talkfest when we walked in. "Sorry to spoil your conversation," I said, "but I think Kathy still has some work to do."

I explained the situation to Kathy who nodded agreement. She closed her eyes and was soon deeply relaxed. When Athena came through, she spoke directly to Balbir. "Yes, Balbir, you do have a spirit nearby, but it is a helpful one. It is a Spirit Guide who loves you very much. In your youth you were close friends, but he died in a car accident. He was quite spiritual as well as intelligent. In his lifetime he tried to help you understand important things about God. Unfortunately, you were only interested in the material world.

"He has now returned from the Light with vast knowledge. He knows what great good you can do and that you have been given special gifts. He has been quite persistent in following you because he is still hoping that you'll listen. To make certain that you know he is with you, he is allowing you to have glimpses of him more and more often. If this upsets you, you can, of course, send him away. But he does love you."

Athena paused. Balbir sat with his head down, his hand in front of his face. Was he hiding tears? No one spoke. Finally, Balbir gave a huge sigh and groaned, "I can't believe he's here. But it is such a distraction! There is always something up there. I can see it in the upper corner of my eye."

Silence.

Then, he said: "Yes, I know who it is. We were very close. I liked to party and always changed the subject whenever he became serious. When he died, it was..." Balbir's voice broke and it was a minute before he could go on. "He was like a brother to me... maybe closer than a brother. I mourned a long time after his death." Another deep sigh. "Well, I'm glad it's not a dark spirit, but couldn't he stop bugging me this way? It's REALLY annoying!"

After a short silence, Athena asked, "Do you want to send him away... this brother. This one who loves you?"

In an anguished voice, Balbir cried, "No, I can't. But find out what he wants from me. This is driving me crazy."

"He just wants you to listen. He will lead you to the right teachers. He got you here, didn't he? This is a beginning. You will always have free will, Balbir."

Now, looking much smaller than his six-foot frame, Balbir nodded. "Yes, it's a miracle that we are here. Thank you, Athena, for all your help. I will try to start listening. I have made myself so busy that it was impossible for anything but the material to get through to me. I have business interests all over the world and I travel a lot. It has kept my mind quite occupied. But yes, I will... apparently, I MUST... start listening."

The main work was done and, after Kathy "returned," we all talked quietly for awhile. Balbir's sister woke up and was able to get up and walk by herself. She still looked groggy but was able to function. This was vital since the family was to leave for India in three days, except for Melissa who was staying home with their children. From India, Balbir was to visit other countries where he had business interests. He would be gone at least a month.

"I know you don't have much time," I told them, "but we really like to do some follow-up therapy if at all possible. There is always a great deal of pain to work through from situations which occurred while the attachments influenced you. With hypnotherapy, your subconscious will quickly recall the times when there was trauma and it can be released. It is very effective in balancing a person. But see how your time goes."

With such a long trip ahead, I didn't actually expect to see them again. Their visit had taken over four hours and now that they were ready to leave, we felt well acquainted. Although hugging was not in their culture, they let Kathy hug everyone and wish them well. The sister gave us a weak smile but looked completely confused. Obviously, she had no idea what had happened, but she was able to walk out without help. The rest of the family beamed with happiness and Kathy and I felt very fulfilled.

When the door closed, we joyfully sat down to say a prayer of thanksgiving to God, Jesus, Michael, the Angels, Guides and all the helpers.

Kathy left and, later that evening, much to my surprise, I got a call from Balbir. He talked excitedly as he told me how pleased he was with our session. He had called Dr. Kay as soon as he got home and the doctor advised him to return for the additional work suggested before they left for India. They had plans for tomorrow, but could Kathy and I take them the following day? Balbir was especially anxious to be able to talk to Athena again. We made a tentative appointment if Kathy was available. She was and said she looked forward to the meeting.

It was quite a different group that came on Friday. The sister had gotten some sleep but still looked exhausted. The other family members exchanged greetings like we were all old friends.

It was agreed that I would work with the sister in my office while Kathy stayed in front with the others. After explaining our work more in detail, she would channel Athena for Balbir.

For our second session, I do what is called "healing the child within." As I slowly take a hypnotized person back in time, they remember traumas. Since we have worked before, the person usually goes into a much deeper state and clearly recalls past events. Over half remember when they were babies. Then they are led back into the womb where they feel contented in this warm, dark place. At times they sense they are not wanted or that there is arguing about them. They may express sorrow that they are going to be born.

I encourage "infants" to go back further in time and remember when they were with spiritual counselors deciding what their soul's purpose was to be. Usually they perceive at least three spirits. I encourage them. "Now see what your soul's purpose is. Ask them?"

I get many answers, but "love" is most often stated. I hear: "To grow in love," or "To open myself to love."

After returning to the womb and recalling details of their birth, I have them feel their body. As they remember growing older, I stop when they come to an age where something greatly disturbed them. I ask their present day self to go back mentally and hold and take care of the younger one. The mature adult comforts the child and, eventually, there is forgiveness and the dissolving of anger. It is an effective and quick way to melt trauma. If it has been extremely horrible, of course, I may need to return to certain scenes in future sessions and work on them some more.

Healing the past is what I had planned for Balbir's sister. Also, dissolving any resentment against the man who had sent the evil spirit to her was important. I briefly explained what I would be doing and got her consent. She was used to having dental patients and easily relaxed in our reclining chair.

All went well for about fifteen minutes and then her extreme fatigue set in. Suddenly, she was in a deep, deep sleep. She began breathing heavily and snoring lightly. As a rule I prefer not to take clients when they are in a state of exhaustion, but in this case, I felt I had no choice. I tried every technique that I could think of to arouse her but nothing worked. She was totally OUT.

I put the recorder on "pause" while I prayed for a minute about my dilemma. Finally, I decided to go ahead as if she were awake. Since the subconscious never sleeps, it would follow my directions. She would have the tape to listen to when she got home and then could experience everything again.

For some time I had planned to make a generic recording to aid the "child within" for those who could not come to my office.

Now seemed the perfect time. Speaking directly into the recorder, I went through the whole program as if she were involved. With no response, it was a strange feeling, but I continued.

When I finished, I went out to the others and explained what had happened. Since I was to work with Balbir next, they wanted to come and carry her out. "No, no. Just clear some space on the couch for her. Have mother be ready to help her," I told them.

I went back to the office, called her name and took her

hand. "You are now going to get up and go out to see your mother," I gently commanded about three times. "Get up. I will lead you out."

She never opened her eyes but moved and, with my help, was able to get out of the chair. Walking backward, I led her to the front room. "Your mother is now going to take you and give you a big hug," I said as I passed her hands to her mother's. She hugged and then was easily led to the couch where she plopped down and continued in her deep sleep. Everyone stood around, talking in amazement, but she never stirred.

Balbir and I went into the office and, in about ninety minutes, were able to accomplish much deep work. After his hypnosis, he was able to clearly see how he had avoided looking at many events in his life. "It's like a hundred pound weight has been lifted off me," he said with a big smile.

When we returned to the front room, his sister was awake but dazed. Again, she sat there quietly, although totally confused about what had happened. The family was in high spirits at that point and I gathered she must have felt that everything was okay.

Kathy had been with them while I was working and, by channeling Athena, had answered many questions for Balbir. Kathy had made everyone comfortable and feeling at home. We all hugged warmly as they got ready to leave. We had been involved in a deep and personal experience which knocked down the normal barriers which strangers have.

We learned later that the sister was back at work and doing well, but we've not seen her since. There was a long interval before we saw the rest of the family.

After they left, Kathy sat down with a bewildered expression. She can be quite psychic at times and was picking up unusual feelings. "I have such a strong connection to that family. I don't understand it. They are from a different country; a different culture; a different religion. From my background, I shouldn't have anything in common with them. Yet, I feel a tremendously strong spiritual bond. It's like we're related. I know I'll see them again."

"Well, they're leaving for India tomorrow," I replied. "It may be a long wait." It was.

In the following months, I was led to start teaching *How To Talk To Your Angel* classes. They were well received and I had anywhere from six to eighteen at a class. At the end of the day, I spent about ten minutes explaining *Spirit Release Therapy* and another short period on how people can protect themselves from wandering spirits. It was from these classes that the core of what would become *The Soul Workers* evolved.

For a growing number of students and clients, I was sending an occasional newsletter about classes and activities at our Healing Center. I had sent a letter to Balbir and his wife on occasion but had never had a reply. It was nearly two years since I had seen them and it was about time to take them off my mailing list. For some reason, I decided to send a "last one."

Much to my surprise, Balbir called. After pleasantries were exchanged he said he wanted to come to my next Angel class. He said he had been traveling extensively, mostly in Asia, and had gone to many remote places to learn from gurus and high holy persons. "I'll tell you all about it when we get together," he promised.

After saying that I looked forward to seeing him, he asked about Kathy and was disappointed to learn that she was not going to be at the Angel class. He had hoped to talk to Kathy and Athena.

On the day of the class I was shocked when he came in. He had not been robust, exactly, but now he was so extremely thin that he looked like a high wind would carry him away. He even seemed shorter than I remembered him. He was dressed in neat, casual clothes and carried a large set of prayer beads, the type that Hindus sometimes carry. His greeting was friendly though he seemed a bit distant and had an air of humility about him.

I noticed that he sat in the last row and over in the corner. During the class I tried to get audience participation, but he sat there quietly and said nothing. There was no facial expression so I had no idea whether he was agreeing, disagreeing or even if he was enjoying the group.

In the morning, after introductions, class members share any personal Angel experiences they have had. I explain the difference between Angels and Guides and then teach them various meditation techniques. As the day progresses, the students communicate on a deeper level with their Angels and have a stronger appreciation for them.

When we broke for lunch, I learned that Balbir did not plan to join us. "I am a strict vegetarian now and I eat only one meal a day," he told me. He laughed at my concerned look and quickly added, "Don't worry, I'm fine. I'm really used to it now and am not at all hungry." He continued.

For much of the past two years, my Spirit Guide has led me to many places and many studies. In cities, and in the most remote places that you can imagine, I have met an amazing array of teachers. Each contributed something to my spiritual growth and understanding. I have had to make many changes and accept as truth many new ideas. Believe me, I am not the same Balbir you met here before.

"I have accepted my spiritual mission here on earth. Indeed, as even you saw, I can't do anything else. I had been swimming upstream against a swift current. Now I just go with the flow and say and do whatever I hear my Angels and

Guides tell me to. I don't fight it anymore. It's been very rewarding. I am one of the most richly blessed persons on the planet. Not in just a material way, but in every way you can think of."

Balbir's face shone while he talked and I could see that he was indeed peaceful and happy. He was a far different person from the anguished soul I had seen two years before.

When we returned to our class, I asked if there were questions or comments. Balbir volunteered and spoke to the group: "I have been on a long journey of many thousands of miles to learn about spiritual truths and how the spirits help us. I came here today to see if the information was the same. I am happy to tell you that it is."

Then, with great emphasis, he added:

You are very fortunate to be able to come here and receive most important understanding about the spirit world. I had to climb high mountains and wait days to see spiritual teachers who could enlighten me. You don't have to do that. It is here for you. You can not learn it all today or even in a lifetime. But, as Dr. Joy says, there is much available for you to study and there are many books you can learn from.

The salvation of the world truly rests on our working with our Angels and Guides. They are most anxious to lead us to the higher planes. We cannot ignore this material world, but we can rise above it to help all of mankind. When you are ready, you will receive the information you need. People will be brought to you that you can learn from, or whom you are destined to teach. As you learn you will, in turn, become a teacher to others. It is all in Divine Order. Our free will is always honored, but I can assure you from

my own experience that life is much happier when you get
into the Divine flow. You have a purpose here."

When Balbir finished, we all sat stunned for a moment. I finally broke the silence to thank him and agreed that our free will would not be interfered with. I reiterated the idea that the Spirit world was most anxious that we open ourselves to spiritual direction.

Later, when we broke into small groups, Balbir became quite animated and eager to assist anyone who had questions. Not many men usually attend Angel classes, but that day, there were several and Balbir was able to give them some excellent guidance. It was a great day altogether and everyone left on a "spiritual high" with plans to meditate more and connect with their Angels.

I thanked Balbir again for coming, sharing his experiences and helping to spiritually enlighten the group. He assured me that we would be seeing more of each other. And so it was. The "student" had returned and was now a teacher.

CHAPTER 6

Fire! Fire! Get Out!

*M*embers of The Soul Workers' Group are not zipping around the world all the time like Balbir does, but we do seem to travel a lot. We are always eager to go somewhere for a new seminar or conference or to hear an important speaker. We have an insatiable interest in many of the exciting topics that are being presented these days.

It is amazing that even our vacation trips often become great learning experiences. For instance, our educator, Jill, came back to The Group with a remarkable story after she and her husband, Mike, took a three day mini-vacation to a large Canadian city.

They were staying in a mid-town hotel and getting ready to go out to dinner, when the fire alarms started a loud whine. Jill and Mike were startled at first, but then began to laugh. "Just a false alarm, I'm sure. This hotel may be a little old, but it is certainly solidly built."

They continued dressing until there was the sudden sound of someone running down the hallway, pounding on doors and yelling, "Fire! Fire! Get out!"

Almost simultaneously they heard the clanging of fire engines racing closer and closer. Fear washed over them like a cold shower as they ran to the window. Jill shouted, "They are coming here! We've got to get out!"

Looking down from their seventh story window, they agreed that they didn't want to have to climb out and jump into a fire net. Memories of The *Towering Inferno* flooded their panic-stricken minds as they scooped up a few things and headed for the door.

Small curls of smoke were creeping into the hallway as they ran out. Several others were already out there. "We can't use the elevators. Where are the stairs?" they screamed at each other. They all looked frantically around but could see no "EXIT" sign. "We have to go down the stairs!" they kept repeating.

As everyone was milling around, frantically looking down different hallways, Jill paused to take a slow, deep breath and whisper to herself, "Love is letting go of fear; love is letting go of fear. Dear Lord, please send help. Blessed Angels, get us out of here."

She felt a sense of release relaxing her tense body. It was then that she noticed a tall, nicely dressed man casually leaning against the wall. He was looking at his watch, which seemed bizarre under the circumstances.

The tall man looked at Jill and said, "Follow me. I'll lead you out." The words were said in a calm, quiet voice and then he turned and made his way down the hall. He moved quickly but didn't run or seem in a great hurry.

Jill and Mike felt a great sense of confidence in this stranger and called to the others, "This way! We can get out this way!"

Like a milling herd of frightened cattle, the group quickly formed into lines behind Jill and Mike. Almost at once they were at a stairway and started down. The smoke was a little thicker here and many started coughing. With the smoke and panic, some were having trouble breathing.

"Cover your nose and mouth and breathe slowly!" ordered the tall man in a loud voice. Like puppets on a string, everyone immediately took a handkerchief or part of their clothing to cover their nose and filter out the smoke.

Jill and Mike grabbed the railing with one hand and kept part of their faces covered with the other. More people were desperately crowding onto the stairs as they reached each new level. It had the potential for being a disaster if anyone in the nervous crowd tripped and fell, but the group moved smoothly and calmly as they quietly followed the leader.

Jill suddenly felt like she was almost gliding down as the floors quickly passed. She began praying aloud and, even though her voice was muffled by the cloth, she realized that others were joining her when she heard them also praying and an occasional "Amen."

All at once they found themselves in the hallway at ground level. As they rushed through the open door and into the wonderful clear air, helping hands pulled them along so that those behind would not be held up. "Move forward quickly," a bullhorn kept repeating as everyone stumbled out.

As soon as they were a short distance away from the burning building, Mike stopped and said, "Where's that man? We've got to thank him. He may have saved our lives."

The others who had followed them out were still grouped together in a semi-shock state. "Did you see what happened to the man who led us out?" Mike asked.

"What man?" most of them said. Only the couple who had been right behind Jill and Mike had seen him. The four started to search the crowd for him, but there was no trace. Because he was so tall and dressed so well, it seemed he should have easily stood out.

They were interrupted by a harried young lady from the hotel who was trying to herd everyone toward a table set up in the parking lot. "Everyone who just came out of the hotel… please go over and report in," she said. "We MUST account for everyone."

Still looking for their rescuer, Jill and Mike tightly held hands and made their way to the table. A policeman and fireman took down their names and then asked how they got out of the hotel. Jill began to explain what happened while Mike continued to glance over the milling crowd.

"Just the four of us saw him," she said as she finished her story. "We'd really like to thank him. He was so calm. That gave us a real sense of confidence."

"What's going on?" Jill wondered to herself as she saw the policeman and fireman look at each other and break into broad grins. Finally, in a somewhat sheepish voice, one said, "Well, miss, you may not believe this, but we think it was an Angel who saved you. This happens quite a bit with fires and accidents. We don't think you'll find him. Just thank your Creator for sending him."

Jill and Mike began to laugh. "Yes, we know about Angels. They sure do show up everywhere. And, thank heaven that they do!"

"Hey, have I got an Angel story for you," Jill exclaimed at the next meeting of *The Soul Workers*. She excitedly told about her adventure and then ended with a puzzled, "Only I can't figure out why he was looking at his watch. What do you think?"

Everyone thought for a minute and then someone suggested, "Maybe he was waiting to see how long it would take before someone thought to pray. Didn't you say you didn't see him until after you prayed, Jill?"

"Yes, that's so. But Angels don't care about time. I can't figure out why he was even wearing a watch. Hmm. Maybe he wasn't. Maybe he was just looking down and waiting. Well, it's a mystery."

Jill's story brought up some questions. When teaching *How To Talk to Your Angel* classes, I had made it simple, "Angels are messengers from God who have never had bodies. Guides have had bodies, but now that they are in spirit, they are allowed to help humans at times if they choose."

I really thought that was all there was to it since I hadn't begun to understand just how complicated it gets in the celestial realm.

Angels told us that spirits have a much finer vibration than we humans (or those in the third dimension as they call us), which is why most of us can't see them. There is the analogy to a fan which spins so fast we can't see the individual blades, although we can feel the effect.

But can Angels slow themselves down enough so that they can take on the form of a human and be seen? And is this different from the ghostly apparitions of deceased humans? And what about Guides? After hearing Jill's story, I decided to find some answers by asking Johnna to channel Angel Samora when I visited her. Johnna had three broken bones in her foot from an auto accident and wasn't going anyplace, so she welcomed company.

We had met when she attended one of my lectures the year before. A recently graduated massage therapist, Johnna was a short, bouncy dynamo of human energy. She had had many jobs before joining the natural health field and now, seeing all the possibilities, she was like a sponge soaking up information.

While she was taking one of my courses, I spent a brief period explaining *Spirit Release Therapy*. Her eyes widened and sparkled as she exclaimed, "I've got to know more about this!"

She quickly joined the class of *Soul Workers* which was then forming.

During the following weeks, as she went through the hypnotherapy sessions, she had some remarkable experiences and life-changing releases. In addition, she not only had her Guardian Angel speak through her, but also a fantastic *Soul Worker* Angel who called herself Samora. Since we were rarely seeing Kathy because of her mounting home obligations, it was exciting to have another Angel who understood our work.

Just as Johnna was the opposite of the laid back Kathy, so Samora was a much different personality than Angel Athena. The latter had a soft, gentle way of speaking that enfolded you in love. Samora was also loving, but she communicated with a greater intensity and, at times, spoke so rapidly that we could hardly follow her. As dynamic as Johnna is, I have never heard her talk that fast. I began to see that Angels all have their individual personalities, just as humans do. Despite the differences, Samora's information was as deep and inspiring as Athena's and it wasn't long before she was assisting us with some of our clients and giving us needed insights.

Johnna was still relatively shy, at that point. So, after some weeks, when I understood that it was time for Samora to "go public," I didn't tell our delightful channel. It was during a *Talk To Your Angel* class that I casually announced that we had a new Angel who was most helpful and would enjoy talking to everyone. Johnna was stunned and most reluctant, but with the group waiting, she finally came to the front. I ignored her "I'll get you later" look and started the *Prayer for Protection*. Johnna began taking deep breaths and Samora soon came through her.

While it usually takes Athena three or four minutes to start speaking through Kathy, Samora often starts talking in less than a minute.

At the class, she gave some new information and beautiful ideas about how those in attendance could better communicate with their Guardian Angels. Samora spoke easily and obviously had none of Johnna's reluctance about talking before a group. In fact, she told everyone how delighted she was to be able to share what she knew. Her work was to help spiritualize souls and she was happy whenever someone was open to listening.

After Samora finished by asking God's blessing on everyone, she quickly left. Johnna slowly came out of her trance and then, looking at the audience, flushed with embarrassment. "You did great!" I assured her. "Samora was a joy and most helpful." The appreciative participants agreed by breaking into an applause of assurance that all was indeed well.

There was a medical doctor in the group plus some teachers and therapists. Johnna felt intimidated by all these highly-degreed people but began to regain her composure as she saw that Samora was a "hit." In fact, after the class, several asked for a private reading from Samora.

"You let Pandora out of the box," Johnna frequently told me at later times. How true. Each time Samora gave a "performance," Johnna liked it better. Since Samora seemed to agree, Johnna was eventually giving "Angel readings" at psychic fairs and at any event that involved Angels.

I became more and more sensitive to the necessity for us to always realize that the channeled information was something we had nothing to do with. We agreed to let it come through us, but it was from God's messengers and we must always remember to thank and praise God for the gifts and to never take credit for ourselves.

One day, I asked Simon: "What happens if the ego gets in the way of those of us who channel?"

Ever the pragmatist, Simon's answer was simple. "We weren't with you before; we might not be with you in the future. Continue your prayers of gratitude and stop worrying. All IS in Divine Order."

Yes, of course.

By the time I went to visit Johnna after her car accident, we had been through much together and were close friends. She was an enthusiastic student and was learning quickly in *The Soul Workers'* class. Now, in her small home, we conversed for awhile and then I explained my confusion. Was she up to channeling?

"Oh, yes! It feels so good when Samora's energy comes through," she readily agreed.

It was 92 degrees outside and Johnna had no air conditioning. Still I insisted on turning off the fan so that the noise wouldn't interfere with the tape recorder. I felt sure this was going to be important information. It was.

Johnna drifted into a relaxed state and Samora took over her vocal chords. She already knew my questions and began to answer them. I kept wiggling around to keep from getting stuck to the vinyl kitchen chair as I became progressively warmer. Still I forced myself to stay focused on what she was telling me and tried to keep it all clear.

SAMORA: *Yes, some Angels have had bodies, but it is a special experience for a certain one they are caring for. Or, they may be called for a specific task as in Jill's rescue from the fire. The simplest thing is to ASK for help and we shall be there! We will come in whatever way is needed. You can ask for all the heavenly hosts and KNOW that you will be receiving our help. For we too are just an energy source coming from* [Samora's voice lowered in respect] *the main Power Source you call God.*

An Angel may just appear in your life. One may come for a brief moment or for a week or month or a year and is able to bring you through a difficult crisis. Then it leaves your space and time.

Dr. Joy: Then they go back to being an Angel?

Yes. Remember your soul is on a journey and the proper teacher will be there for you if you ask. It may not be an Angel, but your Angel might gently direct you to the right person or persons. We are like the oars in a boat which help you through the currents of life.

Do we have an Angel in our *Soul Workers'* group?

[Slight pause…] You have those who are most highly connected and are open to receiving spiritual gifts, but none of them are manifested Angels. They are truly a powerful group, but at this time, they are still going through their transition of accepting who they really are. As they raise their consciousness, each day their power will be heightened. They are now working through their fears but one day will be able to do the healing as Jesus did — as He promised others could.

They'll be happy to hear this, I'm sure. And now, Samora, what about Guides?

The difference between a Guide and an Angel is the vibrational frequency. Also, Angels are closer to the eternal knowledge of our God energy source and so have a better understanding of what is happening within the Universe.

A Guide is someone who has transformed from physical energy, that is a human body, to spiritual energies. By choosing to aid humans, the Guide is also helping itself to raise its vibrational frequencies to a higher learning plane. As a spirit, you are just in a different classroom, but always striving to raise yourself to a higher plane and learning unconditional love. Whether in body or spirit, the past must always be released so that it does not jeopardize your growth NOW. Humans do not usually understand that ALL of us — Angels, Guides and mortals — must continue on our ascension path toward our Creator. There is always room for more growth.

So, basically, the difference is that an Angel is a messenger from God and we have a straight-line connection as it were. We receive the Almighty knowing and, if necessary, can use the Power to create the experience you are now wondering about.

So, some people we meet could really be Angels?

Yes!

We are truly meeting Angels unaware at times?

Yes!

Does this happen often, or...

Frequently!

Can you give me any idea of how extensive this is? Are there a million here now?

There are no numbers to any of this.

"Of course," I murmured, realizing that it was a dumb question. They are apparently coming and going all the time. Besides, talking to Angels about numbers is almost as useless as talking to them about time or space. Our man-made concepts don't work in the spiritual realm. So, I continued with a different thought.

Dr. Joy: Do Angels come and go when they take a body? Or, do they stay with that one body?

SAMORA: *Angels have different duties. I use the word "duty" since humans understand that they all have different functions. Athena, [Kathy's Angel] whom you know, and I work on soul issues, but all have specific purposes. It could be one is here to help with a difficult relationship, another to help heal, another to aid in prayer requests that have been made, etc. If it seems essential to slow down vibrations and take a body for a time, it can be done. God loves you with an unbelievable and unconditional love. He sends His Angels to care for you. And we do.*

Thank you, Samora, that explains a lot. But what about Spirit Guides? Must they go through Angels and then to Source to get their information?

Guides do not necessarily go through Angels for they are like you, going through experiences on their soul's journey. A Guide is like a grandmother talking to a grandchild, giving them the wisdom that they have accumulated. They freely pass it on. But, as you have said, be cautious about what Guide you are picking up. At times you can channel into a Spirit or entity that is not as wise as another. Be careful with whom you connect! Realize that a Guide will give you their best information, but it may not all be the best for you. When you are tuning in and experiencing different spirit energies, test that it is good for you. Do I make myself clear?

Yes, thank you, we'll try to always be aware that we must test Spirits. But it seems that a person may have a Guide and then, after certain progress, they are given a higher or more advanced Guide.

Yes, this is so. You will find that it is like you are going through a college, a school, and you move from teacher to teacher. Some may have the same Guide all their lives. Others may grow and be ready to pull in and accept the wisdom of their Higher Self, such as Kathy, Balbir and Johnna who have allowed themselves to be open to receive and to hear. In this way they are able to connect with the higher energy frequencies so that they can bring back the information to share. They are examples of what many are doing in and around the Universe.

I see. And what about my Guide, Simon, whom I understand is a Master Teacher.

Simon is most wise and brings much inspiration, but I don't know what definition many will put on "Master Teacher." You keep the learning and wisdom acquired in your lifetime. Simon is like a Professor of Knowledge; he loved to learn and to understand and to share when he was on earth. He has continued this through the centuries. Because he was an avid reader and experiencer in his lifetime, it allowed him to absorb much knowledge about many things and now, on his present learning level of experience, he is still absorbing vast amounts of knowledge. He is in a realm now that you are not in because you are caught in your third dimension. Where he is, he can freely connect with higher realms and he chooses to filter this information to you when you ask.

I gathered this "filtering" was necessary since, as humans, we cannot begin to understand the scope of the material Simon is acquiring as a celestial "gadabout." Even though it must seem like he is talking to kindergarteners, he is always patient in explaining things to those who ask. One time, he confided that while living on earth, whenever he came back to his home in England, after traveling on the continent, he loved to share all he learned. He even taught women. He said this laughingly and with mock horror as though that was something men wouldn't consider doing back in Elizabethan times. It obviously appealed to his whimsical nature to be doing something that was not standard custom for his day.

Having received Samora's answers to our questions about Guides and Angels, we then asked about various individuals. She was as helpful as she could be, but at times, reminded us again that we were in the land of free will and we would have to wait for people to make up their minds about certain things.

One of the people we asked about was Philip, a young medical doctor from the Middle East, who joined our *Soul Workers' Group* at times. He was very interested in holistic health and spiritual work. He tried to visit us when he could, but his long hours of work and study often prevented him from attending. Because he would someday have wide influence as a physician, I allowed him to come whenever he could. Still, I was concerned because he wasn't truly trained as a *Soul Worker* and no others had been permitted to come. I decided to ask Samora about Dr. Phil and she provided the following insight.

If not part of The Group, it will be for his own healing process so that he can take what he is learning into the practice that he will be doing. Happily, he is open and receptive. It is going to take the efforts of many young persons to bring science and spirituality together. Even though he has a piece of paper that calls him a healer of great knowledge [referring to his M.D. degree], *he is still a young man working through his own fears and insecurities. He needs the strength and reassurance which he gets from your Group. The information that he is saturated with just by sitting in the healing presence of the energies that are magnetically attracted through to him, is going to make him a much more powerful healer in his own right. He will be brought into better balance and, at a future date, will be able to implement much of what he has been learning into his own practice.*

He will always bring good into the Group even though he is not completely a part of it. It will always be a plus for all.

I'm glad to hear that. Now what about the meeting of Dr. Phil and Balbir that has been suggested. Would that be a benefit for one or both of them?

[Another long pause while Samora seemed to be checking out the situation.] *Both. Each time there is a thought that two should meet, there is a reason. Balbir has a special ability to help raise and uplift and cast off many things which have been transfixed upon a soul.*

Each time something is given, something is given back. So when Balbir, or any healer, helps another, you get in return. Maybe not at the moment, but the Universe shall supply much. The union, therefore, can only be most beneficial to both.

This sounds great. Should Johnna and I be there, so you and Simon can channel through?

It would be a good idea. It would be a help to all. Much information is going to be brought through.

We thanked Samora again and thought about what might happen when Balbir met Phil. I thankfully turned the fan back on while Johnna re-entered the present dimension. Her foot had been forgotten while she channeled and she was happy and at peace as I left her.

SIMON, Dr. Joy's Guide

ANGEL ATHENA, Channeled by Kathy

ANGEL SAMORA, *Channeled by Johnna*

ANGEL DAVID, Channeled by Balbir

CHAPTER 7

A New Kind Of Spirit

*A*bout two weeks later, Johnna, Kathy and I met Dr. Phil at the impressive home of Balbir and his gentle wife, Melissa. Everywhere there were exquisite reminders of Balbir's worldwide travels. Vases, sculpture and artwork had all been brought back at one time or another. Melissa's talent for arranging and decorating were obvious. All the more so, because guests felt comfortable in the surroundings.

Kathy and Johnna had finally met a short time before and, immediately, it was like they were lifelong friends. Their Angels, Athena and Samora, were both *Soul Workers*, had spent much time together and had great love for one another. It was the beginning of our understanding that spirits have close bonds of friendship, just as humans do.

We spent some time helping Balbir and Melissa get acquainted with Phil. We were not sure why we were all to be together, so we made small talk. At first we thought that world-traveler Balbir was to give some advice to the young doctor, but soon, we felt something else going on. We sensed that we had spiritual visitors and they had something they wanted to tell us.

After channeling for awhile, you become aware when your Angel or Guide wants to come through. It is different with everyone, but the Spirits have ways of letting you know.

We all grew quiet as we understood that this was to be a night of channeling. Balbir's mouth started to tremble, (one of the ways he knows when there is a spirit message) and he closed his eyes in meditation. Without saying anything, the rest of us looked toward Kathy to lead an opening prayer. She gently accepted and began:

> *Dear Father/Mother God: Help us to remember that we are here to be truly helpful; that we are here to represent You Who sent us. We ask that we may be daily channels for Your Blessings for each and everyone that we meet. Tonight we ask that the words be Yours and not ours and that we may be voices for You. We do not know what to say or do, but we have faith that we will be guided at this time.*
>
> *We wish to give thanks for each and every one that You have sent to Guide us… and to our Guardian Angels. We are content to be where we are for we know You are with us; that the Light of God surrounds us; the Love of God enfolds us; the Power of God protects us and the Presence of God watches over us. We know that wherever we are, God is and all will be truly well. For this, we give thanks. Amen.*

By the time Kathy finished her prayer, Balbir was breathing deeply as he tried to keep himself grounded while the vibrations of a high Spirit came through him. He often channeled an advanced being who called himself David, but sometimes others came. The rest of us are aware when our channeled Spirit is coming because of certain subtle feelings we get, but none of us has the extreme physical manifestations that Balbir does. If you aren't familiar with his actions, you wonder if he is having a heart attack.

He still had his eyes closed and we calmly waited for him to speak — except for Phil who had never witnessed this before and, being a doctor, nervously wondered if he should do something. I motioned to him that it was okay and he settled back into his chair. Suddenly, I was surprised to sense that Samora was there and ready to speak through Johnna. I turned toward her and began our communication.

Dr. Joy: Good evening, Samora.

SAMORA: *Good evening. You always know when I'm here, don't you?* [There was a smile in her voice as she seemed pleased that she was recognized.]

Yes, I always seem to know. Johnna's face becomes so relaxed that she appears different. We're so glad to have you with us on this auspicious occasion when we're all together in this lovely place. We're not sure why we're here, but we know we'll be given helpful information.

This is an important evening and you will hear much, but first I've been asked to make a request of you. When you say the prayer for protection, would you please end with "And all is in Divine Order?" It is hoped this will constantly remind you that all that happens IS in Divine Order. Know that all that is happening is not your idea, but is your willingness to carry out the wishes of the Divine.

I see everyone is nodding in agreement. We are pleased that you have agreed to try and remember to do this.

Tonight will be an education for all, for all will be experiencing and noticing different and new things. If you will be aware of what is happening around you, you will notice your feelings will be much lighter. *If you close your eyes, you will feel as if your whole essence is lifting for that IS what is happening. At this moment, your cellular structures within your souls are being enlightened.*

This is also true for our young doctor friend who is going on a new spiritual journey. He has asked to be included in this holistic fashion of what life is truly all about. For, in order to have the whole essence of truth, Spirit must be added to the formula. So, now he will experience the love which is the true essence of himself in order to know that Divine Love, which is the essence of all that is, and is the healer of the soul, the mind and the body.

(This seemed very much in line with past messages which indicated that the Angels and Guides were to help with bringing Spirituality and Science together on the planet.)

Samora's voice began to fade after only expressing a few thoughts and I said, "Thank you, Samora. Are you supposed to be relaying the message that seems to be coming through Balbir or is another Spirit coming?"

I shall speak for myself.

We were somewhat startled as a strong masculine voice came through Johnna. I timidly asked, "What is your name, please?"

I am David.

"Oh, yes, Balbir's guide. Thank you for coming."

No one asked why he wasn't speaking through Balbir because we were only intent on getting the message.

DAVID: *You are wondering why you are asked to come together at various times. It is for you to experience the channels of energy that* come through these human souls. At different times in your lives, you have all agreed to help bring Divine Will to the planet. That is why we come to give you much information, but more important, is the energy Source. More than from our words, you will experience a fluctuation within yourselves that will uplift your spirits and enliven your minds and allow your bodies to come to a better balance so that you may experience life in a less frustrating manner. Each of you here uses too much frustration in your existence, even those of you who think they have everything under control.

Yours is a peace mission. You are on earth to help bring harmony and balance to the souls, the minds and the bodies of other humans. If you look at the education and experience of those in this room, you can see each has a special gift to give to mankind. Sense that which is happening, for you are being enlivened. The energies which are here are blessing each one of you so that you can move forward in steady fashion and bring the messages out into the world. Each of you will be going to different sections of the world. Each one of you will be going on different journeys to help. In the near future there will be a net of minds and the expansion of the energy called Love, all around the globe. The world will become saturated with Love.*

You, my dear Philip, are going to be learning in a new fashion. It is your education, but also your special abilities, that will be coming forward to give you new insights into the way of healing. There is much that you are going to be able to transform as you take what you have learned of the physical sciences and add the principles of Spirit. Take what you already know and allow your psychic energies to empower you, to reclaim that which you truly are. You have many messages

---

* Two years later: Phil is studying in China and Balbir is going to new countries — and a new continent — on his business travels which frequently involve him in spiritual work. Kathy, unexpectedly, spent some weeks in Europe and has been in other places where she was needed. Johnna has traveled but remains Michigan based. My husband and I moved to Tennessee over a year ago.

which you yourself can bring the world. But you are still looking for a guided path and think you need to be looking. You do not need to be looking; you need to be experiencing that which is already within yourself.

Balbir, even though this message is not coming through you this time, it is meant for your ears. You are doing a very good job in utilizing your energies to the fullest potential that there can be. You are a gifted soul who is helping those around you. You bring much peace to your friends, but they bring much peace, joy and help to you also. The rejoining of old souls is going to bring much peace and happiness to you and your family.

Melissa, my love, you are the spirit queen of this household. Know that you have all the many blessings that you surely rightly deserve. Even though you claim you are on the physical path, you have never left the spiritual. The spirit of your essence is all around us. You are a queen bee.

There is much that is going to be coming forth, even for my friend, Johnna, whom I now speak through. She sits here in a joy of this feeling and experiences the energies which flow through her for they are all healing. She asks — you all ask — why certain things happen. Faith and trust are the energies that make miracles and that is the frequency for the many blessings and healing rays which are coming at this time. As each of you have your frequencies aligned within your whole system, you will be able to receive the information to know why you are here.

The enchantment that you feel (and enchantment is a fun word, is it not?) for you are all enjoying this situation which has brought you from every corner of the world. Yet you are able to sit here in the "now" and wonder why you are all together. You have been brought together as a synergistic movement to help make all the pieces of the puzzle into a whole. That is, you have more strength in being and working together than separately. You are like radio waves and later *you can help empower each other, even from a distance.*

We in the Spirit world are very grateful to you for your willingness and we wish you to know we are here not only to help but to serve. As you go about your tasks, your soul is receiving many wonderful merits so that it can move forward to its highest potential.

David gave us further personal messages and then said he now opened himself for us to speak to him. We were quiet for a moment — probably dazed — and then I continued the conversation.

Dr. Joy: Thank you for your help, but I am trying to understand what you are saying about the "net of minds." I visualize a big net which seems to go all around the world. Each of the humans who is helping is a part of it and we appear to be holding the hand of the one next to us. By coming together there is a synergy of strength, and Light comes from each point where two or more are joined. Is this correct?

DAVID: *Yes.*

And this net that I see — does it cover the world?

It is like a grid all around. All humans are an extension of one another because you are joined by the Light of your Creator. You are always united. Even though the physical may not be together, your energies, your thought patterns, are always united. You are like radio waves, always in tune with one another. As you consciously unite in mind, you empower one another; you help to bring balance to that which is within you.

I began to see why we are always warned about watching what we think. Negative thoughts can affect others. I presumed to ask another question.

So, are you saying that by this channeling, this is even helping Johnna's broken foot to be healed?

YES! This is why I am with this one. When you have one of the highest forces in the Universe flowing through, it cannot help but heal. If you will all now be still, you can feel the existence of higher energies within and around yourselves.

We all paused for a long while, trying to experience what David was telling us. Finally, he spoke again.

Philip, you CAN take this in. Experience that which you are feeling. There is an advanced soul within yourself that you have allowed to lie dormant. It is an old programmed reflex that you deny your inner thoughts. There is within you, as with Balbir, a great goddess of wisdom. It is the goddess (feminine) side of you that has been suppressed that must now come forward. Within your heritage lies these wisdoms that have been held repressed. There is a new movement of these energies for they are moving toward the Higher Essences of what Spirit is all about. Allow these gentler feelings to move through you and experience that which you truly are.

Philip: How can I really feel that which seems like real pain when I am blocked with fear?

'Tis your choice. Change your choice. You are in charge of your feeling nature and all you have to do is re-choose. I cannot make it any simpler. Something that is so simple can be so difficult. It is like the vehicle of Faith; it does not carry you if you do not allow it to. It is all in the allowance.

You've come to the planet of free will and it is your will, your energy, that is stopping you from moving through this curtain — and it is only a curtain with slits — that you must just go through. You've just stopped at what seems like a barrier.

Master your own feeling nature. Stay in peace. Forgive. Do not fester upon what "was;" move forward to what "is." If you have questions, go within. Go within to your Higher Self for answers.

David gave us other information and then Samora was back.

She reiterated that Phil's interest in the Holistic-Spiritual way was good and that he should continue learning, as he will then be one step ahead of the many others who will be coming to this understanding.

SAMORA: *There is much wisdom in what you have learned [in Medical School]. All that you have learned is not wrong. It just needs some new understandings and balances that will make it a better way of utilizing talents. So, it would be wise to continue learning more from books, classes or being with other healers of like mind.*

Philip: What about direction?

Follow your heart for when you follow the energy of your heart you are usually following and finding your truth pathway. Does that make sense?

Yes, but it seems there are so many different ways to go. How do I know which one?

[Samora, sounding somewhat impatient…] *Claim one! Then see if it is the right one. Until you start, you have nothing. If it doesn't feel right, then go on to the next one. If you are in the middle of a pool, put one arm in front of the other and start swimming or you will never get to the end. Take one day at a time! That is all you have. You don't* have tomorrow or next year, but you are putting all your energy into it. Focus on today. Grab something you think you may want. If you have five things on your plate, you will starve if you spend all your time trying to decide which to eat. Choose one!

What about relationships?

You push relationships away because you are afraid of having a relationship with self. Until you get "self" taken care of, you cannot attract someone to yourself because you do not feel worthy of having anything. You do not even feel worthy of claiming something you feel you may want because you're afraid of which one to grab on to. So, how do you expect someone to grab onto you when you're afraid to put out your hand to be grabbed on to?

So, I should work on myself first?

That's right! You are attracting exactly that which you want. It all comes back to choice. Somewhere there are twists and turns and you have to decide which way to go. You cannot move forward if you do not put one foot out. If you make the wrong choice, at least you have moved.

People cannot make choices for you. They can give advice, but… YOU… must make the decisions. You do not have to do anything except what you feel is best for you. Your parents gave you life, but they cannot direct you now that you are a man. Just because you came from a culture which expected you to follow the directions given by your parents does not mean that should continue throughout your life. Cut your own path. Many others have this path in their heritage and they either allow it to hold them back or it encourages them to go forward on their own. It all comes back to the matter of choice.

You were taught to doubt, that you were not wise enough to make decisions for yourself and that is a lie. You are a competent person.

Keep saying "I am a competent person and able to make decisions in my life" and you will do fine.

Phil sat in silent thought, and after a period, I decided to ask a personal question. Although I had developed some of the spiritual gifts, I still had not made much progress on my feeling nature. I had been working on the issue but knew there was much more that needed to be done. "Samora, you know I need to feel more. Can you give me some ideas on how to go about it?"

She promptly replied, with a little chiding. "Do it through visualization. You who have all this education must know that what you implant within your visual and feeling nature goes through your whole system. Visualize and it will be so."

Her voice then changed to a slow, creepy tone, "At this moment, feel a spider walking upon your arm. Feel the sensation of each one of its legs as they hit the nerve endings within your arm. A tickle, a frightening, scary feeling perhaps as this monster crawls up your arm. You can experience a feeling as this creature walks upon your skin. Can you not?"

"Oh, yes!"

"You're feeling," she replied in a matter-of-fact tone. "Now change the feeling from fear to love."

What an assignment! I closed my eyes and thought for a moment until I was able to say, "I changed the spider to baby Jesus. We all can feel love for babies. I took this love and transferred it to the spider. Now it does not seem scary."

SAMORA: *Very good. Keep working and it will come. Now, you have been wondering about some other things. What do you need to know?*

Dr. Joy: Well, one thing that keeps coming up is the "Ascended Masters." I am always coming across some reference to them. Just who are they?

I will use "he," but it can be anyone. An Ascended Master is one who has learned to stay in peace amongst the turmoils of life and has ascended himself to a high place where he is now working directly with God. He does not allow the dishevelment of life to destroy his peace. So you, and all who are around you, may work to ascend to that space where you are in perfect peace.

So, is this what they're writing about when they speak of the Ascension of man?

Yes, it is when you have moved your emotions from the anxieties, angers and frustrations of life so that you do not react to their destructive vibrations. You ascend yourself to a place where you are moving along with the flow and do not stop this flow to fester upon a situation. YOU may ascend to peace. The more you allow yourself to stay in peace, the higher you shall ascend. Master your own feeling nature is what you are told. Stay in peace. Forgive. Do not dwell upon that which was, but look forward to what is now.

That's an even harder assignment, I decided. Well, let's try another subject.

Sometimes people come to talk to my Guide, Simon, about a loved one who has died. He asks them to think about the person so that, through their vibration, they can be found. If the deceased has gone to the Light recently, they may send a message of Love, but if they are resting they are not allowed to come back. Those who have been in the Light (Heaven) for some time may be able to come back and give words of peace to their loved one. They say how happy they are and this is consoling. Other times, the spirit is still earthbound, and with the loved one's permission, Soul Angels are sent to bring a message of love to the deceased one. The Angels then encourage the person to go to the Light with them. It has resulted in many souls being released from their earthly bondage. The people who come leave with a great sense of peace and joy.

I was happy about this, but at times, I felt unsure of communicating with the dead. In asking Samora, I worded my question poorly.

Is it helpful to call on the spirits of those who died to come and talk to those who were close to them in life?

SAMORA: It can be, but why not just call on your Higher Self [Holy Spirit] and move straight through to the Central Core. Why go to those who are still on their journey when you have all you need to know within yourself? Go within. Trust thyself. Even though these others are no longer on a human dimension, they still do not have all understanding. You have more if you tune in to your Guiding Light. You will get clearer, straighter answers about what is good for you.

Realizing she misunderstood the question, I tried again. "What I'm saying is that sometimes it gives comfort to people to know that their loved ones are happy. This is especially true for those who do not understand the afterlife. Getting a message or, in some cases, actually sensing a departed one's presence can be most consoling."

Since this was helpful to people, Samora apparently did not see that this should even be a question. She just kept with her former idea as she replied, "Yes, that's fine, but if you are looking for answers or information, go within to your Higher Self."

Sometimes I have found it difficult to get the right answer from Angels if they are not clear about the question. And forget about asking them about something that has to do with time. They are in eternity where time does not exist.

Following her answer, Samora gave individual messages of encouragement and love to each of us and said, "Goodbye for now."

"Thank you, Samora. You always give us much wisdom. We love you, too," the group replied.

When she finished, Balbir was still breathing deeply as he had been since the channeling started. He occasionally trembled and made small moaning sounds. He did look like a person in deep distress. "He's really in ecstasy, there is so much love in the higher vibrations," said Kathy who had seen him like this on other occasions.

"I think there's another Spirit trying to come through," I suggested. "Let's try." Looking at Balbir, I said, "Good evening. Is this David again?"

A deep voice began in a slow, staccato monotone, "I am not David. I have come to make contact and to give counsel. I have been observing and now choose to participate in this venture."

"Thank you for coming. Will you give us your name, please?"

There was a long pause and then the voice continued in its slow, deliberate way, as though it was difficult for him to talk.

I do not have reference to a name. I come from a different galaxy of existence that operates only with thought processes. Words are foreign to us. I come from a very spiritually-evolved system and we have been participating in the evolvement of what is now happening in your world.

I am capable — and able — to observe and speak to the one you call David. Also, I can converse with the spirits who channel through the highly-spiritual souls who have gathered here. We will be involved with the counseling that will be done as we grow in our union together. The dialogues will become easier for there will be many messages given through different ones within your group. Much information shall be given and you shall record it.

We want you to know that we are here to help and to guide. You are very spiritual persons and we choose to be part of it all. Please call upon us again.

Anxious to not let this one slip away, I hurriedly said, "Thank you. We appreciate your coming, but we don't know how to call you since you don't have a name. Don't you use any names?"

Please give me one. I shall respond for, I will just know when you shall call upon me.

This was certainly a new kind of spirit. What was here?

Dr. Joy: Are you what we would call an ET or Extraterrestrial who has come here in a space ship? Or are you without a material body?

We do not have the same kind of existence as you or what you call ETs. We are more in spirit form. There are many more types of existence than physical forms. You and your other humans have just not learned all there is to life forms as of yet.

In what ways could you be of help to us? By giving advice to us personally or for telling us ways we can help others.

Yes to both of those. We are a clan of great healers. There is much information we can guide through to you to make what you call "your job" much easier. We have a vast amount of knowledge that we will be happy to share.

Will we be able to hear you in our mind. How will you communicate?

I shall speak through those in your group or through the human system I am now using.

So, you would speak through me or through others in our *Soul Workers' Group*?

If it is required, but they must have their body prepared for I, like David, am a very high energy source. Their bodies must be prepared for what will come through them.

How do we prepare our bodies?

Your Angel or Guide partners can tell you, for there is a process that you must go through to allow your bodies to raise in vibration. You must also be able to just release yourself and let the flow of energy come through you without question.

We all were thinking about these unusual statements from this new type of being and started to ask another question but were interrupted by a voice from Johnna, "He is gone."

"Gone?" I echoed in some confusion. "Oh, we would have liked to hear more. Is this David back again?"

"No, this is Samora."

"Oh, good," I exclaimed, happy to have a familiar Spirit with us. "What was that all about?"

SAMORA: *This was a lesson for all of you. There will be transitions [messages] coming from other spaces in the universe bringing much information. As your group grows, it is going to be channeling much healing energy. I know we keep being extremely vague, but you are having all you can do to handle what you have now. One day at a time.*

Dr. Joy: That's true, Samora. We are doing our best just to keep up with all the new knowledge that keeps coming our way. But this one who just came through — he was in the shadow of David. If he has a sense of humor, can we call him 'Shadow?'

Fine. He is not particular. Names mean nothing to him. I am hearing the name George. It is simple and basic; not a particularly fancy name, but it is what I am hearing and it may give you something to work with.

I think you may realize that the energies here are flowing very smoothly and easily between all of you now. You have become more used to and accepting of spirit world visits. You no longer have to struggle to freely accept what comes. By the time higher energies, like George, come to you, you will be readier for the higher voltage. We are most pleased that the flow is going so smoothly.

I am going to leave you now for you all have many things to think about and ponder upon. There have been more things happening here today than you have been consciously aware of. When you are among these various energies, it enlivens each cell within your system. Before you sleep tonight, ask your subconscious to bring to your consciousness a way to connect you to the higher being of knowledge. You each have one. Go within to your inner self. Do not deny your inner voice. Trust that it is real. Goodbye for now.

We all thanked Samora again and spent the rest of the evening discussing what it all meant. There truly was much to ponder.

CHAPTER 8

Soul Rescue In Vietnam

*D*uring my eight years of *Spirit Release* work, some really incredible stories have come through clients. It has not only been satisfying to help them, but to know that so many souls have been released from their earthly prison. *The Soul Workers* and I were concerned, however, that we could only help one living person at a time and it was obvious that there were millions of earthbound souls who needed releasing, some attached, some not.

There had to be other ways to help many. The Angels assured us that there were. So, when Balbir told us the following story of what happened to him in Vietnam, we were all ecstatic. Now we knew that, with the help of the Angels, there were ways in which humans could work with Spiritual forces and many, many souls could go to the Light… return to God… all at one time.

Balbir's worldwide business interests require him to leave the U.S. three or four times a year to check on everything, and do some troubleshooting and/or expansion work. In March, 1994, while on his travels, he spent five remarkable days in

Vietnam. This was our conversation.

BALBIR: *I have had no business interests in Vietnam but Ken, my associate in Singapore, lived there for about a year two or three years ago. For some time, he had been telling me about the opportunities there and the last time I was with him, I said, "Hey, we should go to Vietnam the next time I come. Please, make all the arrangements." In retrospect I can see that I was directed by my Spirit Guide to say that.*

By 1988, the Vietnamese began to open up to the rest of the world, as they were anxious for foreign capital to help rebuild their war torn country. In 1989, many foreign firms were going in and Ken went there, representing an Indonesian firm.

Since I now work closely with Ken, I felt his knowledge of Vietnam could be beneficial in starting a business venture there. However, when Kathy and I had a channeling session before I left, the Angel Athena let me know that this was NOT to be a business trip but a spiritual mission. Vietnam needed soul help and I was to be an instrument through which the Angels could work. I only had to go there. All the other arrangements would be made by spiritual forces.

The words that came through Kathy were: "A new beginning must take place in Vietnam for that country needs to be healed. A LOT of healing needs to take place. One thing that must be done is to help release the earthbound souls. There are many. [We were not given any numbers but just understood that there were a great many.] Because of the war and the traumatic deaths they suffered, many souls remain earthbound; unable to find their way to their Heavenly Home."

Helping these souls was to be one of our tasks. Another was to transmit healing energy into the country, into Mother Earth, the land... as well as into the people. So, in this way, the pain and agony that Vietnam as a whole was carrying, and the people were carrying, would start to be changed. A new beginning and progress could then take place.

I was stunned at the instructions because I did NOT know if it was in me to do such an awesome assignment. The Angel told me: "Don't worry! Just go there. You will meet certain people and everything will fall into place."

Before leaving on my trip, I was told that the release would start taking place on the third day of my trip at 10 p.m. So, at exactly 10 o'clock, I was to meditate and ask for Divine help to accomplish our task. This would be 11 a.m. Michigan time. This is when Kathy, and the Soul Workers she contacted, would be praying on this side of the world. This would provide us with the balance I needed to receive the high vibrations of the Angels.

I could not explain all this to Ken, so I didn't try. I just told him, "We may have a task to do in Vietnam. I'll tell you about it after we arrive." I never told him exactly what it was because I wasn't sure myself how it would come about.

Dr. Joy: Is Ken spiritual?

No, not very. He is a rather worldly person but a good man. Ken made all the arrangements for us to go to Vietnam from Singapore after I finished my business there. He also planned for us to meet with a friend of his and that is when everything began to fall into place.

Ken's friend, Thomas, is Singaporian, has lived in Vietnam for six years and is married to a Vietnamese lady. Since Chinese is quite common in Vietnam and Thomas is Chinese, his wife speaks that language. I also speak Chinese, so the communication gap was bridged. We got along wonderfully and soon became friends.

I'm mentioning Thomas' wife, Sng, now because later I discovered she was going to be a part of our work. I didn't know that when we met and were getting acquainted.

What part of Vietnam were you in?

HoChiMin City (Saigon), which is in South Vietnam. After the country opened up to businesses in '88, the Taiwanese were the first to go in, which is another reason so many speak Chinese. The Taiwanese are the biggest foreign investors there and control a large sector of the investment and financing business.

When Ken and I arrived, we were basically tourists and our hosts showed us around the city. Then it was suggested that we go to a popular resort north of HoChiMin called Vu Tau. It's a coastal town on the South China Sea, which used to be an American R & R beach resort. That sounded interesting and we decided to go.

The whole plan fell into place so fantastically easy that it is difficult to explain. Thomas arranged a mini-bus and a driver for us and I asked him and Sng and their family to come along. Her father wanted to come and her brother and sister thought they would like to join us. So, suddenly, we had a party of seven going to Vu Tau. This was all absolutely unexpected and not originally planned by us. The Angels must have made the arrangements.

We made the journey to Vu Tau where Thomas had booked chalets, or cottages, for us. I decided that was a good place to spend this special night, for it was the day agreed upon to do the work that my Guide had been preparing for.

We arrived in the afternoon, rested and walked along the beach. By then I knew Sng was to be a helper in our spiritual task. This was a delicate matter, but over dinner, I asked Thomas if it was okay for his wife to come to my room at 9:30 p.m. and join us in prayer and meditation. Surprisingly, he not only didn't object, he told her, almost commanded, "You go to Balbir's room at 9:30 p.m. He is going to say some prayers. You go with him." She agreed.

We are often encouraged to have a trinity of three people and so I knew we needed someone else. I invited Ken to join us and, even *though he didn't know what it was all about, he accepted. My next step was to ask Sng to go and buy three white candles at a local shop. I should explain that, since I have been so involved in this Soul Work for the past year, instructions come to me very clearly as to what is to be done next. It isn't like hearing a voice. It just comes to me instinctively and I know what I'm supposed to do. It is almost like I am physically forced to do it. If I am supposed to say something, it is pushed out of my mouth. If I'm to do something, it's understood to "Do it!" and I set out to do it. Instructions are very clear and I don't fight it any more. I just follow directions and everything works out.*

Anyway, when Sng got back with the candles, everyone else had gone to their own cottages. This left us free to get together. Ken and Sng joined me and waited for me to start, not knowing what to expect.

Did Ken think this was quite strange?

Ken and I were college classmates in Canada fifteen years ago and we have worked closely together in our business for the last three years. He knows me quite well.

He has not been inclined to go in your new spiritual direction though?

He has seen the changes in me and we have discussed a few spiritual matters. He is not surprised at what I do any more but just accepts what I suggest.

We lit the candles and I explained a little of what to expect. I didn't know exactly what would happen myself. I asked them to pray in their own way with me for a half-hour and not to be surprised or frightened if physical changes occurred in my body. As you know, when the higher Spirits come in, there can be bodily changes and sounds. I must constantly work at grounding myself. Channeled words may come through, but I did not expect that this time. After warning them, we all settled down and became quiet.

Thomas, Sng and I started meditating at 9:30 p.m. After a half-hour, I felt the Angels taking over my body. I clearly remember opening my eyes and it was 10 o'clock sharp. I have three different Angels who come to me and I have some idea who is with me from the vibrations I feel. For this important occasion, it felt like all three. There may have been even more.

I felt my body shaking as the lighter vibrations of the spirits took over my whole physical structure. Ken and Sng couldn't help but feel frightened, they told me later, even though I had warned them. They just sat there at first, paralyzed by what they saw. It's one thing to hear about it and quite another to actually experience it and hear the sounds that often come from me.

Then, the energies of love began to pass through me in stronger and stronger waves of pure joy and ecstasy. As the vibrations got stronger, I reached out for their hands. I felt I had to further ground myself or else my body might lift up. My breathing was as deep as if I had just run a mile. But, through this, I managed to get them to hold hands so that we were in a circle. As the vibrations went out my right hand and around the circle to come back into my left, I encouraged them to send energy into the ground. In this way, the healing energies went into the earth, purifying and restoring it.

The others felt my vibrations, of course, and it was a high physiological experience for all of us. Never having experienced anything like this, they felt compelled to go along with whatever was happening. It was also surprising to me that I was able to do this with people who were strangers to Soul work. However, I wasn't given time to feel uncomfortable about it. When things are happening, you just hang on for dear life. Of course, it is such a feeling of being totally enfolded by Divine Love that I didn't want to let go.

Then there was a startling climax to the whole event. Grounding myself and pushing and blowing the Love into the ground took quite a long time. Then, suddenly, it was like I was pulling in the whole world. I could hear a loud noise coming from myself, like "Ffooth" that went on and on and on. I felt like all my internal organs were being filled to the bursting point. I was aware that I was pulling the souls... the earthbound entities into myself through my mouth. There were thousands... a great multitude.

From all over Vietnam?

From all over. Very High Energy Sources (Angelic) were involved. After breathing in for what seemed like a long time, my head was pulled back so that it was tilted upward and I blew everything out with a loud "Wooosh!" This inhaling and blowing out lasted for at least 20 minutes. I kept trying to concentrate on grounding so levitation wouldn't take place. When I felt my body starting to rise, then I concentrated on stopping it.

When you work to ground yourself, do you use the technique of thinking of roots going into the earth from your feet or do you use something else?

That's the method I use. Before I started Soul work, and before hearing about it in your Angel class even, the book, Ask Your Angels,[1] was given to me. When I got to the part about the grounding techniques, I heard a voice saying this was what I had to learn and practice. I read a little, but had to put the book away because I started on one of my world travels. Every city I went to, I spent time meditating and started with the grounding process. I was always hearing instructions. For two months, even after I returned home, I practiced grounding before I began my meditation. Then the higher vibrations started coming to me. Even with the two months of training, I had difficulties in aligning myself with the vibrational forms. They varied, depending on who I was channeling. The Angels work hard with a person before giving the powers that are needed for high Soul work.

I believe Soul Rescue is the job of Warrior Angels and some of the Angels who came to me were Warriors. Their responsibility is to get souls to the Light... back to God.

When we speak about Spiritual Warriors, we are usually talking about St. Michael and his group. Are these the same as the ones you are talking about?

Different ethnic and spiritual beliefs have different names. The name I was given is David. Names are not really important, however. It's whatever you are comfortable with.

So, this blowing out was like you were sending earth-bound souls toward the Angels who were gathering them and accompanying them to the Light. I understand that souls cannot go alone, but why is a human necessary? Why did they need you?

It's hard to understand some things that happen on the spiritual level but it seems that since these souls had physical bodies, living physical people must pray for them and intercede for them. In the half hour I was meditating, I was asking for help for all these poor souls.

I see. I know that some Churches believe strongly in praying for a soul after a person dies. This may definitely be valid. It seems that being Earthbound may be equivalent to what some consider purgatory, certainly not a happy stage until they look up and go toward the Light. Balbir, did you get a sense of how many souls were rescued that night?

About three years ago, before I had agreed to do this work... and before I came to see you… I was involved in my first release… which I thought was to be the only one. At that time I was given the gift of seeing souls being rescued. Now I can see souls leaving a person and I have seen up to a thousand. That night there were so many that I couldn't tell, but I sensed thousands… probably tens of thousands.

So, it all happened in your room in that short period?

My main work was done, but the Angels continued in their task throughout the night. In the U.S., Kathy and the other Soul Workers were praying for Angelic help to be sent to me, those working with me and all of Vietnam.

When I returned home, I heard that Angel Athena (who was helping with this whole uplifting) came with another Angel and asked for Light and Love to be sent to all of the countries on earth and then to the whole Universe. So, even though we started with one country, this beautiful help was sent throughout the Universe. It was fantastic!

So, what happened after you finished the work in your room?

It was about 11:30 p.m. and we went to the French cafe to join the others and eat.

Everything was open that late?

Oh, yes. Remember, Vietnam was a French colony for 150 years. There are still signs of their influence. Vu Tau was a resort area and, while the country is ancient, it is becoming quite modern and successful. It was almost 1:00 a.m. before we got to bed. Then, the next event happened. At 4:30 in the morning, I was awakened. I felt a strong message coming and knew that we were to go to the beach for the sunrise. I woke up Ken and, half asleep, he followed me out of the room.

I knew we had to go and observe the rising of the sun because that would be the culmination of the whole task. The Angels (probably thousands of them) had been working all night to get the last of the souls to Heaven. At sunrise they would be through and it would be a great new beginning for Vietnam. A joyous new day!

[At this point, I could only say, **"Wonderful."**]

Ken and I started for the beach when I realized that we needed Sng, the third part of our trinity. That posed a problem because I didn't know which cottage the women were in. So, I just went around banging on doors and waking everyone up. "Come to the beach for the sunrise," was my only excuse. Much to my amazement, instead of objecting or getting angry, everyone agreed. A whole group of sleepy-eyed tourists stumbled down to the beach in the dark. We sat on the sand facing the East for almost an hour. During this time, I was feeling heavy Angelic vibrations, but it was too dim for anyone to notice.

Suddenly, the sun peeked over the horizon and everyone cheered as if they were at a big party... which they were. I was under Angelic control at this time and, when the sun's rays hit us as a group, a gigantic cry escaped from my throat as I faced the East. The only way I can describe it is like an earsplitting roar of victory and total joy. My assumption is that the Angels, with David as their leader, were expressing their exhilaration and delight that the task was completed.

There weren't many on the beach at 5:30 in the morning and those who came down didn't know if it was me shouting or someone just being funny. So, then everyone went back to bed and I spent some quiet time in thanksgiving. It was such a fulfilling time. I was just in awe.

Then what happened?

After the work was done, Ken and Sng were given special

blessings and rewards. Because Sng was chosen for this work, I was able to tell her what her role in life is, what her future holds and what benefits her family would receive because of her participation. Her brothers, sisters and all the members of her family will have everything they need and will be taken care of, is the message I heard. I put my hand on her forehead and the vibrations that were sent into her body helped cleanse it and bring up her level of spirituality.

During the next two days, while we were visiting various places in the mini-bus, I was able to channel much helpful information for all those journeying with us. Ken asked about his mother who had died just the year before. We received messages from her and also encouraging words about his daughter who would be blessed as a reward for his help. So, even though it is not asked for, many benefits come to those who do the Lord's work.

This is one of the most profound revelations I have observed in my work. If people assist me when I have a Divine task, they receive many blessings from our Creator. The benefits are often given immediately. It is most satisfying but also humbling. It is a great encouragement to me for accepting His work... which often includes large challenges.

Most of those traveling with us were not told about what happened in the room that night, but still everyone was blessed. Family problems, health concerns, the future... all kinds of questions came up. The Angels were able to give information and guidance and, sometimes, actual help.

The Vietnam journey was a most uplifting experience and, now that I'm back, I can only encourage others to listen to their Inner Guides, their Angels and to do the Lord's work. You will be directed. You do not have to give up your employment for there is work to be done wherever you are.

Thank you, Balbir, for your inspiring story.

CHAPTER 9

Different Methods & Protection...
Including "Do It Yourself"

ar from trying to duplicate Balbir's dramatic episodes, I use and teach Dr. Baldwin's *Spirit Release* techniques in which we work with clients in person whenever possible. However, there are many other methods which seem to produce beneficial results. For instance, Rev. Eugene Maurey, in his book, *Exorcism,*[1] explains how to clear a spirit-possessed person from a distance. He claims that he can clear as many as fifty people a week with prayer and by using a pendulum to get responses. It seems to be a practical method for him as he writes about many remarkable healings as a result of spirit releasing.

He feels it is better and safer not to be in the room with the client. If the person is psychotic, his point is well-founded. In such cases, working remotely is obviously wise. Rev. Maurey considers many insane to be spirit possessed. He does not believe there is a demonic so I assume that he has missed them or he has found some pretty strange earthbound spirits.

In *Exorcism*, Rev. Maurey quotes one man as saying he just requests his spirit guides to take care of the situation since they are skilled in the work. He feels they can quickly pick up an earthbound spirit, the work is done and he doesn't get further involved.[2]

This is an excellent idea for those concerned about someone but who have not had Spirit Release training. I suggest this method: Go into a prayerful state, ask for protection and request that God send some Soul Angels to the person you have in mind. Ask for him or her to be released from any possessing entities. Then, relax and mentally see the person as totally well and happy. End by thanking God for all His gifts.

It's extremely simple, but there is no reason why it shouldn't work. The problem is that the person may be in need of some counseling or advice, especially if they suddenly feel quite different. For instance, if a person who is alcoholic abruptly loses the desire to drink, he may be confused and need to find new friends and develop new habits. This is a concern with remote depossessions, but it should not stop the process. (See end of book on how to obtain remote *Spirit Release* information.)

Aloa Starr, who wrote *Prisoners of Earth — Psychic Possess ion and Its Release*,[3] also does remote releasing and uses a pendulum. Her method is different from Rev. Maurey's in that she requires a picture or handwriting sample from anyone she assists. She has taught her method to others and, with these helpers, they have had many successes.

In her book she has an interesting chapter on "Poltergeists, Demons, and Elementals" which sheds light on some of the other things a *Soul Worker* might find around living humans. She describes the Poltergeists as being "unruly, mischievous entities who delight in playing pranks."

They sound like ghosts because they are not actually attached to a living person. They can be found in a home, car or place of business, according to Aloa. They can also be attached to a person's aura. Are they bored ghosts? Who knows. Sometimes, it is not necessary to define all the spirits we rescue for heaven.

Some strange behavior might be explained by the presence of spirits. For instance, Aloa describes elementals as "nature spirits on earth (elves, fairies, gnomes), air (sylphs), fire (salamanders), and water (undines)." While I was somewhat aware of these, I had not considered them necessary to deal with. Perhaps, they need to be.

Aloa wrote, "Somehow one of these little invisible beings of the second density can become attached to one of the inner bodies of a human, usually the emotional. They can be very mischievous and make a child difficult to handle. Almost always they attach to children, possibly because children are so much closer to nature… [they] can also attach to or enter animals, making them act strange and abnormal."[4]

I corresponded with Aloa Starr and eventually visited her in her home in Sedona, Arizona. She has a special spirituality. She is also a delicate, well-dressed, refined lady who is far from what anyone would think of as an "Exorcist." We joyfully exchanged many ideas since we use different methods. She made me more aware of the importance of asking for Angelic help to clear a person's home and aura as well as the actual person.

She showed me how, after prayer, she works with a chart and a small pendulum. Although her method is somewhat different from Rev. Maurey's, she is also able to tell many wonderful stories about how people's lives have changed after being cleared.

It seems that the intention is more important than the methodology. It's actually the Soul Worker Angels, who have been assigned to this work and are proficient at it, who accomplish the task. However, respecting free will, they need permission to perform their job. This we prayerfully ask for. Spirit Releasers who aid others from a distance must first ask permission of a person's High Self. The cardinal rule is to never ever interfere with a person's free will. If the High Self responds "No," the session is stopped.

A minister once said to me, "I just ask Jesus Christ to help with whatever kind of healing or soul work I'm doing. Why would I have to ask Angels?"

"Why are YOU needed?" was my response. "It is because God has given all of us specific jobs — Angels AND humans. When we pray to God or Allah or Jesus, it's like calling 9-1-1. We can't expect the person taking the message to rush over. It's relayed to those who are properly trained for the situation. I'm not usually asking for a medic to come if I'm reporting a fire."

God has billions of Angels trained for specific jobs. The right ones are sent. "He has given His Angels charge over you," is what I understand from scripture. I'm happy we have ministers, but we also need plumbers, teachers, farmers and thousands of other trained people to make this world go around

Carole Sanborn Langlois, author of *Soul Rescue — Help On The Way Home To Spirit*,[5] has quite a different approach to *Spirit Releasement*. This gifted medium is devoted to helping lost souls, or earthbounds, find their way to Heaven. Working with her Spirit Guides, and in a praying support group, she is able to psychically see and hear the soul she is trying to assist.

She writes, "Mediums in many parts of the world have dedicated their lives to helping these lost souls... They allow their bodies to be used as channels through which these souls can manifest. Many [of the souls] will not leave until they have touched the earth plane one last time, for there is something they believe must be said or they need to experience a physical body one more time."[6]

Carole is referring to wandering souls more than to attachments. She goes to "haunted" houses and aids people with many para-normal situations. Hers is a special calling because of the spiritual healing gifts she has received. She has trained many, and perhaps those who sincerely wish to do Soul Releasing can do it her way. While the people I have trained are spiritual, they are not necessarily psychically-gifted. They became adept at the methodology I taught, which was based on my own experiences as well as what I had learned from Dr. Baldwin. Eventually, however, they found their own approach and did releasement in whatever way they were comfortable with.

What is gratifying is that everyone in Spirit Release work is delighted to exchange any information they may have. Coming back from Florida one time, we visited Carole Sanborn Langlois at her sunny Ft. Lauderdale home. Although we had only corresponded, our first reaction on meeting was to hug one another.

An attractive lady and gracious hostess, she was happy to share what she could in the brief time we were together. Then, we channeled for each other and, as always, the messages were most encouraging. When the time came to go, my husband and I hated to leave, but we were thrilled to know that there were Soul Workers in so many places.

Her parting admonition was to always pray for the White Light of protection before starting any spiritual work. I was well aware of the danger of psychic attacks, having worked on others besides Balbir's sister. I agreed that it is important to always remember to ask for protection. In Carole's book, she writes:

"The human psyche is so delicate that it is not something to play around with! Psychic attack really exists and as the negativity gets stronger and stronger on the planet, we all become more vulnerable. When we do this work, we need to keep our shield of protection around us at all times."[7]

Regarding the same concern, Aloa Starr once wrote to me: "There are negative High-Level forces attacking many Lightworkers. Seal your aura twice a day with the Golden White Light. Visualize a mirror-like substance around it so that anything of a negative nature that tries to influence you will immediately be reflected back to itself. We send it back with Divine Love."

Dr. Edith Fiore feels that retaining a strong aura is the way to keep unwanted spirits out. She is probably correct. In *The Unquiet Dead*, she suggests using your imagination to see a brilliant sun inside of your solar plexus. She writes, "This sun is radiating through every atom and cell of your being. It fills you with light to the tips of your fingers, the top of your head, and the soles of your feet. It shines through you and beyond you an arm's length in every direction... creating an aura, a brilliant, dazzling radiant White Light that completely surrounds and protects you from any negativity or harm."[8]

Dr. Fiore writes that once the technique is practiced a few times, it can just be thought into place like flicking on a light. She suggests this should be done twice a day. Although she teaches this method to her clients, her book gives no spiritual basis for it. She may be leaving that up to the reader's personal belief system.

My belief is that this is the highest kind of spiritual work.

For a Spirit Release Therapist to have a trained assistant, or co-worker, to be a "scanner" when searching for attachments can save a great deal of time. By going into self-hypnosis, the scanner can actually "see" into the body of the person they are working on. The therapist then speaks to the various entities who can communicate through the assistant's vocal chords.

Dr. Baldwin's gifted wife, Judith, scans but in a somewhat different way. She keeps her eyes open while putting herself into an altered state. After sketching a human figure on a drawing pad, she marks places where she "sees" attachments. Then, speaking aloud, she gives a short description of what she is clairvoyantly seeing. "There is an old woman in the left shoulder," she may say, or "A dark form is in the solar plexus."

When Judith is not available, Dr. Baldwin finds attachments by having the hypnotized client look inside of him or herself and check to see what or who is present. This method takes longer, but it is also exceedingly accurate.

Our method of working directly with Angels may be unique. When Kathy channels Angel Athena or Johnna her Angel Samora, the human assistant often has little to do except relax and be comfortable. The hypnotist has the job of asking questions and talking to the entities and the Angels. When working for someone remotely, or for someone unable to talk, like Balbir's sister, there are times when I need an entity or demonic to speak so that I am clearer about what is going on. This also allows me to converse with the attachments in order to aid them in understanding their situation better. This is especially true if an earthbound spirit does not realize it is dead.

One time I had a client in trance who was so terrified by the appearance of an evil-looking demonic that he froze and was unable to speak. Fortunately, Johnna was nearby and she came in, saw the situation and quickly put herself into self-hypnosis while I prayed for her protection. As soon as I finished giving the scary one permission to speak through Johnna, but with a stern order that he was not to possess her, her face contorted in rage. In a loud voice, the demon began to scream at me and demand that I leave.

"I'm not going anywhere, but you are," I replied calmly and then went through the usual depossession dialogue. He was a difficult one to convince, but eventually, he expressed sorrow for his actions and left with the Angels.

After the session, when Johnna and our client were in a wakeful state, she began to describe the horrid face and glaring red eyes that she had seen as soon as she went into trance. "That's exactly what I saw!" exclaimed the joyful man, who was now in a relaxed and happy mood and feeling MUCH lighter.

"Well, keep yourself protected so that you don't have any more visitors like that," I laughed. Johnna agreed, "Channeling Samora feels great, but that one was really scary."

Irene Hickman, D.O., a feisty octogenarian from Kriksville, Missouri, said that she has had a great deal of excitement and adventure in her life. But she wrote: "By far the greatest excitement of all my experiences has come in the years since my depossession training. During these years I have been a part of or witnessed transformations in people as possessing entities were removed and sent to 'The Light.' It now appears to me that the possible transformations are limitless. Neither time nor space provide limits. Only the scarcity of trained workers prevents or delays widespread changes in the minds, the health, the emotional tone and behavior of great numbers of people. Let us dream about the possibilities — changes that this therapy can produce."

This is from her book *Remote Depossession*,[9] which she wrote five years after receiving her training from Dr. Baldwin. Although long past retirement age, Dr. Hickman has thrown herself into the work with the zest and zeal of a young convert.

Always a truth searcher, Dr. Hickman began to explore

other methods of doing *Spirit Releasement* soon after she was trained. She also began to question whether suggestion played a part in producing results. Could the changes be due to hypnotic suggestion alone?

To eliminate the possibility, she trained some assistants or "scanners" and began to work on people remotely. Some seemingly miraculous results convinced her that this, indeed, was a valid method and she was involved in "a sacred occupation."

Whenever she speaks in public about Depossession, Dr. Hickman tells this fascinating story, which may be hard to believe.

She heard about four young prisoners, under the age of 30, who had just been judged incurably, criminally insane. The doctors considered them permanently unfit to ever be released.

With the help of a hypnotized scanner, they located the men in a prison over 100 miles away. Working on them, one at a time, they asked for permission from the High Self of each. After receiving permission, they discovered and released both earthbound and dark forms. The behavior of the men changed at once, and within a year, three were released as cured and the fourth was reclassified.

In doing remote work, Dr. Hickman finalizes the session in much the way we do when working in person, only the scanner is substituting for the client. She has her helper find the Light of the target's spirit at the center of their being and visualizes it growing brighter and larger until the entire body is filled with Light. If any area fails to fill, it is necessary to go back and deal with any remaining problem. When the body is filled with Light, directions are given to let the Light expand outward at least an arm's length to form a protective bubble around the person.

When working with a scanner, it is necessary at the end of

the session, to have the person find their own Light and expand it throughout the body. This way, the scanner is also left "squeaky clean."

It was only after working with inner Light for a long time that it finally dawned on me that the Light we are able to see within ourselves is the same one the demons could see. We also are just a spark of God Consciousness. We all are just a thought of God! Satan covers his minions with some dark and red stuff so that they won't know who they truly are. Do we do the same with our bodies? These short-lived physical beings certainly get most of our attention. Perhaps we need to be more conscious of the Light within.

Dr. Hickman found the Release work so satisfying and side effects so non-existent that she proceeded to another idea. She became founder and president of the "Depossession Institute" in 1996. Committees were formed and the plan now is to get like-minded people together to exchange ideas, be a support group and receive additional training from some of the more experienced members. In time, there are to be training sessions for new people and regional gathering in various parts of the United States and Canada. There is also a plan to provide referrals to people who call in for a therapist in their part of the country.

There are now nearly two hundred "Depossession" Institute members and over seventy attended the first conference in April, 1996, in the Chicago area. Participants came from all over the country; one even came from Grand Cayman Island. It was encouraging to find a clergyman and two medical doctors there. The enthusiastic networking seemed to indicate that the organization was needed and would be well supported.

The current address is: The Depossession Institute, Ltd.; P.O. Box 888; Evanston, Illinois 60204.

While the results are impressive — in fact, astounding —

it must be realized that *Spirit Releasement* as a therapy is still in its infancy and is not perfect. In the eight years I have worked in the field, I have seen some great changes in people. With many it is a permanent change; with others it seems to be only temporary as they allow themselves to become infested again. As more people pray and do this work, answers are sure to come. For now, I can only say that I, too, feel it is a sacred occupation and look forward to the time when we provide even more permanent benefits for people.

CHAPTER 10

Dolphins, Whales &
The Environment

*If all the beasts were gone, man would die
from a great loneliness of spirit. Whatever
happens to the beasts soon happens to man.*

– CHIEF SEATTLE

 $\mathcal{F}$ *or some time most humans*
have instinctively felt that there is something special about
whales and dolphins. With the rise in our spiritual consciousness, we recognize that there is a noble quality about whales, the
mammoth denizens of the sea. And dolphins, so personable and
lovable, are noted for often rescuing those in watery perils.
People who swim with the dolphins say that it is one of the most
thrilling experiences of their lives.

Great efforts are still being made to stop whalers from
killing these gentle creatures. They are mammals after all and

not like fish. The same is true for the gregarious dolphins. Boycotts are staged to stop people from eating tuna until fishermen find ways to catch them that no longer include killing dolphins as well.

Saving these impressive cetaceans seems like our "charity" for God's lesser creatures. After all, humans still consider themselves the brains and the center of the universe.

Knowing the human ego, it is with some trepidation that I write what channeled Angels are telling us: we are not the wisest species around. We are still evolving AND have a long way to go. What's more, the whales and dolphins have been saving us for a lot longer than we have been helping them.

Much of this was explained by Johnna's Angel, Samora.

SAMORA: *Dolphins and whales are wise. They help bring balance to the sea where much is being destroyed by man. The sounds they make echo for many miles throughout the water. Because of their loving nature, these echoes help purify the water which is essential for themselves and all other living creatures.*

Water represents your emotional selves and it is important that it be kept clean. As whales gracefully move through the water, the motion of their gigantic tails is like a rocking cradle. Whales once walked the land but went into the sea to become more spiritually evolved. Each generation found it more comfortable to remain in the sea. And so they stayed.

Dr. Joy: I was amazed at how long whales have been on the earth. A construction crew at the NASA Langley Research Center in Virginia discovered a complete set of fossilized remains of a three-and-a-half MILLION-year-old whale. Incredible! But Samora, do whales actually have some connection to mankind?

Like all things, the whales are a part of us. If you could only understand the meaning of the vibrational frequencies that the whales and dolphins put into the water with their sounds! They go deep into the sea. These sounds are very pertinent for the whole survival of your planet.

As the mammals swim through the water, they sing their song and it permeates out like radar and creates a nice balance in the sea. The water is a transmitter. When you make a sound in the water, it creates a wave. Waves are frequencies. Colors are also waves. So, when the whales are singing their song, they're creating a wonderful color frequency. They can put a rainbow into the sea with the pitch of their sound. Colors are sound pitches that you see and sense. So, when you see a rainbow in the sky, you are seeing Angels at work.

You are still not understanding that we work with EVERYTHING! We work with and through whales and dolphins. If we see that something is disturbing the waters, we encourage their song. When their wonderful frequencies begin, they help quiet the problem. They have dispelled many things that could have disrupted the earth.

Song is nothing more than vibrations. Everything is frequency and EVERY THING is frequency. You still haven't got past the belief system that you are not a solid being. You know it in a logical sense, but you do not take it into your belief system.

I know that we're made up of sixty-trillion cells and each cell is a life in itself. But when we look in the mirror, that's not what we see. We don't see cells; we see a solid.

But that doesn't make things different.

So, we see illusions. Everything is vibration and we think we see solids.

You are living in the land of illusion. Nothing is what you see and think it is. You work with your perceptions, not with spiritual reality which is true reality. You keep questioning over and over again. You are like a child who doesn't believe what you hear.

It is difficult to change my thinking to something different from what I have believed all my life. Be patient with humans, Samora, and please tell me more about the dolphins. I understand their brains are bigger than humans' brains.

Dolphins are more intelligent than whales and are more in tune with their spiritual natures. They are perfect spirits in their evolution since they are loving, sincere, joyful, free, accepting and of one mind. Each brood sings out to the others. They are all of one mind, even when separated. Mankind has a long way to go on his evolutionary path.

If Spirit Guides came to help mankind, I'm wondering if any humans have become dolphins or whales. If, after losing their bodies and going to the Light, have any humans chosen to come back to earth as a dolphin or a whale?

Dolphins and whales are a species wonderful unto themselves. They have chosen to be beings of the sea. They don't choose to want to be like you. Mankind has been very cruel to them and to many species, particularly to themselves.

Yes, this is certainly true. As a rule, humans do not see others as a part of themselves. We also have not thought of non-humans as having much intelligence. But in his book, *The Souls of Animals*, Rev. Gary Kowalski writes, "Because all life shares in One Spirit, we can recognize this indwelling beauty in other creatures. Animals, like us, are microcosms. They too care and have feelings; they too dream and create; they too are adventuresome and curious about their world. They too reflect the glory of the whole."

Later, he adds, "In a wonderful and inexpressible way, therefore, God is present in all creatures."[1]

Yes, this is so. It may also surprise you to know that there are insects which are highly intelligent. Even though they are not big nor do they function in the same manner as you, they have a most powerful influence upon your land. They too send out special frequencies that help with creation.

I know many of you are bothered by their pestering ways, but they are here for special reasons also. For instance, the ant is very influential in the structure of your planet. They aren't concerned with Homo sapiens but with the land itself. They see you as a parasite of destruction. They do not view man any more pleasantly than you view them. If they were big enough, they would probably step on you.

Well, I'll try to be careful of them, but I hope they stay out of my house. Lately, we've seen newspaper articles about bees. They are being attacked and diminished by a certain mite and, as a result, many crops are producing very little. It is more confirmation about the inter-connectedness of all things.

But going further down the chain from insects, Samora, what about minerals? I know that there are many in the soil for the plants to absorb so that we get the minerals we need by eating the plants. I realize these are essential for our physical health, but what about the other types of minerals? For instance, some say they feel energy emanating from stones like the amethyst, the lovely violet quartz.

These minerals feed your spiritual nature. You are aware that you have many bodies, but you stay focused on your physical body. The mental, emotional and spiritual bodies, which some see in auras, are much more important. They must all be nourished and nurtured. God has created everything you need.

There are many ways besides food to feed you. It is more important to feed your other natures than to feed the body. A totally attuned person would not even need physical food to survive.

You know that when you hold certain wonderful stones, you can feel the energy from them. You can hold one and, all of a sudden, feel something different as its power surges into you. Angels work with minerals as well as everything else. The more open and receptive you are, the more you will find yourself becoming mentally, emotionally and spiritually attuned.

Samora's words give a whole new understanding to the message that we should pray daily for everyone in the world, for Mother Earth herself and all things on it. Sending love to every creature and asking the Angels for help will bring God's protective energies to assist all living creatures through the many climatic changes that they are now trying to cope with. All animals, as well as humans, feel stress and it affects how they feel and behave.

Some government officials know that the whales and dolphins keep the Earth's eco-system in balance and that they are guardians of the planet. This was written about in the publication *Center of Attention.*[2] The article added, "Please call out to our loving ocean brothers each night and call down the powers of heaven into the ocean."

The Earth Angels have many assignments, one of which is the immense task of making sure the ozone layer doesn't get too thin. They also work at getting enough of the pure air to earth to sustain life for all breathing creatures. If the air gets too dense, many experience severe breathing problems. Some refer to this dense air as ozone.

I became confused about good and bad ozone and consulted a physicist, Dr. David King, a former professor at the University of Tennessee. He explained that the word "ozone" is not always used correctly and there are actually two forms of what is considered ozone.

About twenty-five miles above us, in the ionosphere, ozone is an essential component for shielding us from the sun's damaging ultraviolet (UV) rays. About a mile thick, the ozone layer has been thinning because every day there are about 1,400 TONS of man-made chloroflurocarbons (CFCs) drifting into the atmosphere. A single CFC molecule destroys 100,000 ozone molecules. This is to be remembered if anyone is tempted to use aerosol sprays.

While lightning creates good ozone, there is certainly not enough of it to combat our rapidly thinning protection. On a personal level this means premature skin aging, skin cancers and cataracts.

On a global scale, ozone depletion is part of an earth warming trend which a United Nations panel predicts will eventually melt enough polar cap so that there will be a twenty-inch rise in average sea levels. In North America, a result is likely to be drought and higher temperatures which could cause crop failures. Some of this is already happening.

When coastal regions experience more rainfall and flooding, rivers and soil dry out inland. The UN reports this will cause "an increase in hunger and famine" in parts of Asia, Africa and Latin America. So, being environmentally conscious is a matter of earth preservation. While the U.S. has improved, it still produces over 432,000 TONS of garbage *in one day*.

While there are many environmental concerns, clean air is one of the most important. Bad air depletes our health and our energy. The so-called ozone on earth is really the absence of pure air. At its finest, air can be stimulating, almost intoxicating like a "runner's high."

I understood this better when Sarah, one of the *Soul Workers*, came back and told us about her trip to the Trinity Mountains in California. She had spent a week there studying spiritual healing. She was staying with Crystal Brook, a Native American, and his wife. Suddenly, there was a flash of lightning and distant thunder. They could hear the rustle of leaves as the winds began to rise.

"Let's go!" shouted Crystal. "These mountain storms can be exhilarating." The three of them raced for the car.

As they drove up the mountain, Sarah noticed that in spite of the brisk wind and approaching nightfall, it was getting warmer. Loud claps of thunder, brilliant lightning and high winds surrounded the car, but there was no rain. The clouds were rolling faster when they got to where the mountain trail narrowed and the car could go no further. They quickly got out. As they looked up at the churning skies, they inhaled deeply and began to feel a sensation of energy. "We only have a storm like this every couple of years," Crystal said with excitement in his voice.

"The clouds seemed to spread out like huge wings," Sarah later told the *Soul Workers*. "Underneath there were some sort-of funnel shaped clouds that tapered toward earth. Crystal called them Angels and they certainly looked like Angels to me.

"There was an ozone-like substance drifting toward earth from the heavens. It must have come as a result of the lightning. It seemed to feed us through our pores and enliven us. We started laughing and acting giddy like someone who is high. It was such a joyous, euphoric experience that I felt that must be what it is like in heaven.

"We felt like we could fly we were so energized by the

oxygen. We began to dance around like we were kids. There are certain very pure energies on the mountain all the time and, at that elevation, it is an energy vortex. I always loved the mountain air, but it had never made me silly before. I had never felt anything like this!

"Then — THEN — we saw the purple cloud. I mean PURPLE! [We later heard everyone talking about the purple cloud up on the mountain, so it wasn't just us.] It was still twilight and everything became very intense in color. The greens of the grass and the trees were unbelievably vibrant even though it was almost dark."

After the trio danced around for a few minutes, they decided to meditate for five minutes or so before going back. They sat down on the ground and began to quiet themselves. They prayed that the invigorating air they were absorbing would be for the highest good of all.

Sarah continued her story, "Words cannot express how deeply I was able to meditate. I had a few seconds of fear when I began going really deep within myself, but I just willed the fear away and it dissolved. Suddenly, it was like being lifted into a Divine Connection. It was so wonderful! I have no idea how long we were there, but when I stood up it was as though I had just had eight hours sleep.

"We thanked the Beings or Angels for the wonderful storm and headed back to the house. According to Crystal, the pure air fed even the trees and the rocks. All of nature benefitted from the storm even though there was no rain.

"Since coming to the mountains, I had been asking for the gift of better meditations. I certainly received a wonderful gift!"

Sarah discovered that the ozone, or pure air, had not only rested her and raised her vibrations, but apparently, fed her as well. She said she was thirsty the next day but never hungry. In fact, she didn't eat at all.

That day, while working on others in her healing class, Sarah said she felt her legs and whole body tingle, but her hands were not shaking. "I had no fear about working on people. I had a ton of confidence that I was truly helping them," she enthusiastically exclaimed at the end of her story.

Sarah has worked on me and has such extremely hot, healing hands that I can happily attest to her abilities. If that is how pure air benefits a person, I'm going outside the next time we have a storm! Now I see why Harmony, another *Soul Worker*, gets so excited every time there is a storm. She loves to go outside when there is one and says, "They make me feel so tingly and alive all over!"

She echoes Naturalist John Muir who wrote, "When I heard a storm, I made haste to join it; for in storms, nature always has something extra fine to show us."[3]

Angels say they do not control the weather and the environment, but they try to improve on the problems humans have created. Channeled information is constantly warning us to treat Mother Earth in a sacred way to avoid the major catastrophes humans are causing. Not God! (See Chapter 11: *Are These The End Times?*)

Samora has said, "If mankind does not take the time to advance into a more uplifting spiritual existence, many will be perishing in a way that will look very cruel. This is a time when a better balance must come to Mother Earth. Throughout the world, there are already many problems. For you to help the Earth and yourselves, you must look for balance from within. Each time you bring balance to yourself, you help your neighbors, your loved ones and others to bring balance to themselves.

Be aware that what you express of your feelings is coming from your mind's core. Control your thought process to change your energy and to alter your frequencies. Each word, each thought has either a healing or destructive frequency depending on whether you put a positive or negative frequency into your vibrational core. So, control your thoughts and alter your feeling nature so that the electro-magnetic path you are creating will bring positive frequencies to your home and a healthy vibration to send out to the world."

Realizing that environmental concerns have a spiritual as well as a practical basis, makes us rejoice that world religious leaders are finally planning to be environmentally active. In the summer of 1996, an Associated Press article reported that clerics were holding a religious conference on the environment.[4] While their battle against pollution and environmental destruction seems to be an eleventh-hour effort, it is certainly welcome.

At the conference, the clerics plotted strategies to mobilize their congregations and to create an international network of at least 2,000 "green priests" committed to fostering ecological awareness. At their meetings, the clergy joined with scientists and environmentalists to create a blueprint to raise this awareness worldwide.

Chairman of the Conference, Ecumenical Patriarch Bartholomew, Spiritual Leader of the world's 300 million Orthodox Christians, urged Protestant, Roman Catholic, Orthodox, Jewish and Muslim clerics to work with one another to preserve the environment.

"Unhindered communication among all those concerned is equivalent to the sanctity of prayer," he said on Heyeli, an island off the coast of Istanbul.

Pope John Paul II said the conference could build "understanding of the wonders of God's creation and of our responsibility to care for the work of God's hands."

President Clinton also sent a message to the religious leaders, urging them "to move beyond mere awareness of the environmental crisis toward active and extensive efforts to ensure the health and preservation of the earth."

Father Johannes Geeris, a self-proclaimed "green priest" from New Valamo, Finland, reminded attendees, "If we kill the environment, we will kill ourselves."

So far, man has done an excellent job of killing the environment and Nature is returning the favor with more and more violence. Our Spirit Guides tell us that our concern for our Earth is our salvation and assisting the preservation of all God's creations is truly "equivalent to the sanctity of prayer." The Angels are anxious to assist, but they need our support and our active free will. Again, it is up to us.

CHAPTER 11

Are These The End Times?

The main concern of many is:
What is happening to our planet? There are so many disasters that we wonder if this is the end of the world or the beginning of the thousand years of peace? The answer: it turns out wonderfully, but things will get a great deal worse before they get better.

Some of the channeled information about the next few years encourages a higher spirituality. Other channels give vivid descriptions of destruction which can and might happen. Of course, the direst prophecies can all be altered by bringing "Love and Light" to earth, we are told. So, in a sense, all the information has a similar purpose.

Here is a short summary of a few astonishing "Earth Changes" books, followed by a talk with Simon to clarify some of the more confusing points. I deem these materials valid and hope they will encourage your further reading.

As early as 1934, Grace Cooke in England was receiving magnificent words from an American Indian, White Eagle. Over a twenty-five year period, she channeled several books which all inspire the reader's soul to soar. Among the deeply moving books is *Spiritual Unfoldment*[1] which speaks of the brotherhood of men and angels. White Eagle also tells us about the nature of angels or fairies and claims that all living things began as sparks of life from God and are of the same essence. This book, as well as others from White Eagle, aim at expanding human understanding about the vastness of the spirit world and our place in it. We are also encouraged to work with our Angel friends.

The next uplifting works to appear were *A Course In Miracles*,[2] completed in 1975 and contained in three books with a total of over twelve-hundred pages. They stem from ten years when Dr. Helen Schucman, an atheistic Jew, took dictation from "a voice." Her agnostic co-worker, Dr. William Thetford, typed it up. As scientists and professors of medical psychology, they most definitely did NOT want to be channels. In fact, in the beginning, Helen thought she was going crazy. She was especially upset when she realized "the voice" belonged to Jesus. However, the voice was persistent and she felt compelled to take down the words she heard. During the following years, she came to believe that this was the main work of her life.

The voice began speaking after Doctors Schucman and Thetford, who had conflicting personalities, agreed to "find a better way" to get along. This was the opening for Holy Spirit Who desires to bring all souls into harmony. They were the perfect pair for this formidable work as they did not have to please any organized belief system and were not doing this for any purpose of self gratification. In fact, they kept everything they were doing hidden until the books were completed. Their status as highly intelligent and respected professionals guaranteed that the work would not seem to come from fanatics. It also helped them to meet influential people who, eventually, were able to get the material published.

Now, more than twenty years after the first printing, there are hundreds of small study groups throughout the world; the books have been or are being translated into a dozen other languages and there are probably close to a million copies in print. There has never been any advertising; knowledge of the books has spread by word of mouth. Those who study the books for some time usually feel that only Jesus could possibly have been the author.

The miraculous story of how *A Course* came about and was published can be found in Robert Skutch's *Journey Without Distance*.3

The aim of *A Course* is to bring inner peace, the peace of God. While simple in meaning, it is difficult in living as it frequently espouses such lessons as, "Forgiveness is the key to happiness," and "Love holds no grievances."

The books are often written in first person and, at times, Jesus explains scriptural meanings. Since these are sometimes different from traditional Christian beliefs, many churches curtly dismiss the work as heresy. Thousands of clergy and laity, however, feel that *A Course* answers many spiritual questions. They say the "mysteries" are explained and now their own purpose is clarified.

I asked one Catholic priest, who was studying *A Course*, how he felt about it. He replied, "Oh, it has helped my faith life and my prayer life immensely."

"But can you share it with your fellow priests?" I asked.

He shook his head sadly and answered, "Only rarely."

Many, including some famous people, such as psychiatrist, Dr. Jerry Jampolsky, and author/speaker, Marianne Williamson, have given *A Course* credit for changing their lives for the better.

As *Course* students gain inner peace, they are more joyful, contented people. The books require looking at the world, and everything in it, in a different way. At first, this is difficult for most. After some weeks, however, the ideas become clearer and life much more serene.

What does this have to do with the end times? A *Course* is not concerned about time at all, but only with encouraging each person to let go of fear and replace it with love. This is how the world will become a safer, saner and more forgiving place. The emphasis is on prayer and meditation (listening to God) and realizing that within ourselves is where we will find ALL our answers. In the *Workbook* there are 365 daily lessons. At the end is the prayer, "This holy instant would I give to You. Be You in charge. For I would follow You, certain that Your direction gives me peace."

While Jesus works on getting A *Course* spread around the world, his mother, Mary, appears in numerous places. In the past, amazing miracles have been documented, all the way from Lourdes and Fatima in Europe to Guadalupe in Mexico and Ste. Anne de Beaupre in Canada. These were rare happenings, but now there are reports of her appearing in many countries and to those who believe in one God but are not Christian. Thousands of Muslims saw the Blessed Mother appear several times on top of a Coptic Church in Egypt.

Prior to the fighting in the former Yugoslavia, Mother Mary was making daily appearances to a group of children in the small town of Medjugorie. Hundreds of thousands began making the difficult pilgrimage to this remote village. They are still going and while most are Catholic, there are those of other, or no faith, also making the journey. Friends and neighbors who have gone told me they found a sense of peace there and a deep spiritual feeling unmatched by any other place they had been. Many see the Miracle of the spinning sun and a friend from Colorado told me that afterward the cross on her rosary had turned to gold. There are also miracles of healing and some see Angels.

Mary constantly asks for prayer and penance and, in the past, tried to get the country to avoid the horrors of war. Unfortunately, the deep hatreds erupted and, even though Medjugorie has been protected, the atrocities in Bosnia proved Mary right.

For some time Mary has been said to appear on the 13th of each month in Conyers, Georgia. Recently she has also been seen in a remote spot in the Mojave desert in Southern California. It was reported that three-fourths of the crowd who made the pilgrimage to the area also saw her. She continues with dire earth predictions while pleading for prayer and fasting so that catastrophes can be avoided.

Unfortunately, it usually takes major trauma to bring people to God. In times of war, churches are always full and people pray more earnestly. It must be understood that God DOES NOT CAUSE these disasters. We do. Those Native Americans who are still close to nature, have long warned us, "What people do to the earth, we do to ourselves."

A *Course In Miracles* says that what we do to others, we are doing to ourselves. Scripture says, "As you sow, so shall you reap." In other words, if we treat each other, or Mother Earth, without unconditional love, we must face the consequences. Underground nuclear testing, the vast pollution and toxic chemicals going into the air and the ground, the destruction of trees and rain forests and other desecrations can only mean, the earth MUST heal itself. This will happen with the violence of earthquakes, erupting volcanoes and the furious weather extremes we have been witnessing all over the planet.

More prophecies were revealed in 1991 when Annie

Kirkwood, of Texas, came out with her book, *Mary's Message To The World*,[4] which quickly became a best seller. Mrs. Kirkwood, who was deeply spiritual but did not belong to any church, "heard" Mary in much the way Dr. Schucman had. At first, she maintained that she wasn't Catholic and shouldn't be the one receiving messages. When Mary finally reminded her, "Neither am I," she realized that Mary was Jewish and now is a Universal Mother.

Mary told Annie that she was chosen because of her prayers and meditations and her "pure heart." Also, she was not looking for any kind of fame or acknowledgment. Mary was aware that her messages could not reach the common people through governments or churches so easily as through someone who was sincere and honestly seeking for the truth.

The first chapter of *Mary's Message* repeats the warnings that have been given all along… only with more urgency. The earth changes and wars, which escalated in 1991, will intensify during the next ten years and so the message is for every person on earth. Although the changes will affect everyone in some way, the book provides a message of hope. The more people who pray for the earth and everyone on it and work to bring their spiritual consciousness higher, the fewer catastrophes there will be. If we help people find God in their hearts and minds and evolve into loving beings, peace can reign.

The book has an extraordinary chapter on love.[5] Mary declares, "To bring love and appreciation into your life, there must be a place in your heart where it will be welcomed."

Mary talks of "love energy" and how powerful it is. "Divine Love is an energy force as available as electricity. One day you will be able to send your body on the wings of love."[6] We will be able to travel just with Love Energy? Apparently so.

Can we stop some of the impending disasters from coming

if enough of us join in loving ourselves, one another and the earth? Yes! Will we do it? I don't know.

Mother Mary proclaims: "Make sure you understand that this is not the end, but the beginning of a new era and a new world and a new understanding. The need to prepare is now, right before the birth of this new era."[7]

In the year following *Mary's Message To The World*, at least three other "Earth Changes" books were published. Each book is entirely different, but word rapidly spread about all of them that they were in the "MUST read" category.

The first book, *Black Dawn, Bright Day*[8] by Sun Bear with Wabun Wind concerns Indian Prophecies for the Millennium that "reveal the fate of the Earth." Sun Bear, a Chippewa Indian, received his channeled information in the form of visions and dreams. Like many other modern visionaries, such as Joseph Terelya in Canada and Maria Esperanza in Venezuala, Sun Bear "saw" volcanic eruptions, massive earthquakes, severe hurricanes and tidal waves with coastal flooding.

Sun Bear's book, however, is the best I've seen for offering many practical solutions and down-to-earth advice. He is now deceased but in his lectures and writings, Sun Bear was completely natural but far seeing. While encouraging us to change, he was never slow in blaming white man's mentality for the earth's mess. He complained that for thousands of years Native Americans kept the land in pristine condition, but the white man destroyed it in less than four hundred years. He wrote that his visions "told me there is nothing wrong with the Earth Mother that can't be cured by removing the goofy people who are creating the problems upon her."[9]

Does this mean there will be a great loss of life? Yes, but as people pray to bring up their spiritual consciousness and learn to listen to their inner wisdom which teaches Love, many lives can be saved.

Sun Bear's visions are echoed by many Native Americans who refer to "The Great Purification" that is coming. They know about this from legend and from the ancient native records written in stone (petroglyphs) found in Southwest United States. There are over 15,000 petroglyphs and, according to Indian beliefs, some show major earth changes happening in various places. Sun Bear writes: "After each sequence of events, there is a spiral that means 'and life continues.' This is what I feel also: Life will continue on this planet. There will be human survivors. These human survivors will be the ones who have reached a higher level of consciousness and are willing to move on and take responsibility for themselves and for the planet in a sacred way."[10]

To save the land, and ourselves, Sun Bear encourages a return to simplicity and a respect for Mother Earth and all things on it. He says, "It is a Native philosophy found across the earth that you never kill anything you don't eat; you don't waste anything."[11]

Black Dawn, Bright Day has whole chapters of suggestions on how we must prepare in order to survive "The Great Purification." For those living in areas where the most destruction will be, the direction may be, "Move!"

While many have seen how the contours of the United States may change on the, "I AM AMERICA" map, Sun Bear goes farther and has maps for most of the world. He also gives symbols which indicate what types of disasters or severe problems to expect. In addition to weather and earthquake destruction, there are also indications of epidemics, political unrest, economic chaos, severe pollution, food shortages and other trials. There is a spark of hope given for areas marked with stars which show where there are numerous safe areas. (The

Angels tell us we will be where we are supposed to be.) The predictions for the disasters which are forecast for the end of this century (and have already started) have come from many sources. Geologists believe the stone petroglyphs were made over a period of a thousand years and may be the oldest prophecies we have in the United States.

Nostradamus, who lived in Europe in the sixteenth century, has been chillingly accurate about events for four hundred years. His prophecies for this period of time are similar to those given by Sun Bear. Also giving world predictions was Edgar Cayce, the "Sleeping Prophet" from Virginia Beach, Virginia. His pronouncements about people's health, as well as about events that would happen, proved nearly one-hundred percent accurate. Before his death in 1945, he gave many "readings" about the disasters that could befall the world before the end of the century. They had many similarities to those given by Mary, Sun Bear, Nostradamus and others.

The vital point to remember is: Prophecy CAN change if circumstances change. As we are often told, it is up to us. If we learn to love enough, we CAN change the world.

In 1992, the first of the writings from Kryon appeared. This spirit is neither Angel nor extraterrestrial as we understand them to be. He identifies himself as "Kryon, of magnetic service," and says that, with his helpers, he is adjusting the magnetic grid that surrounds the earth. This is in preparation for the higher consciousness of mankind when we will shift from the third to the FIFTH dimension.

The first book in the series of three, *Kryon, The End Times*,[12] is advertised in an understatement as *New Information for Personal Peace* and *Channeled Teachings Given In Love*. Lee Carroll, the author, was directed to write down the information he heard. A businessman with no metaphysical background,

Carroll felt compelled to start his book with his own nervous outlook on the strange proceedings of being a channel.

Then he writes the words of Kryon which are always loving as he explains that his job is to teach us what we are capable of absorbing about the great complexities of the universe. He is not patronizing but lets us know that, with our existing knowledge, it is like trying to explain intricate machinery to an animal. The reason is that our biological being, our DNA, was tampered with eons ago to keep us from using the vast abilities that are our God-given heritage.

Kryon assures us that we have parts that were not altered including our intuition and our ability to discern. These are magnificent spiritual gifts which we still have, but most consider their intellect more reliable. Not so!

He says, "Your spiritual side is pure and unaffected, and is still intact without restriction. With a balance of the power on your spiritual side, your biological mind and physical body will no longer be limited in scope of understanding. Many of you now call this balance 'enlightenment.'"[13]

Many Angels, Guides and Channels have declared that their grand effort now is to bring Science and Spirituality together to achieve what Kryon calls real science. He says the merger is well underway, but currently we still have only two-dimensional science, not universal science. We must add spiritual understanding as this is where the real power lies.

"You will never achieve sustained space travel without it. You will also never be able to alter or understand gravity, and most important, the transmutation of matter will never be yours without it. Imagine… how would you like to neutralize all your atomic waste, so that a child could play with it, as sand. It's not difficult to do, but it requires skills that you have not yet used, but that you now have the power and permission to develop."[14]

Kryon claims we have enormous raw power resources available to us through the regulated use of our magnetic fields. All the energy we will ever need is here. With us, right now, Kryon likens us to ants sitting on a generator, wishing for electricity.

He explains that as we feed the spiritual longings of our souls, we will experience a gradual change of consciousness which will lead us to peace of mind through the power of Love. With the Love Energy (which Mary also spoke of), we can raise the vibrations of the earth and transmute negativity, which is the absence of enlightenment.

Kryon says that the magnetic fields with which he works are most important for our biology and we should notice that there are negative effects on our health from artificially-created magnetic fields. We have the technology to protect our bodies but rarely do it. He says some diseases are found only in our affluent Western society which has developed many artificial magnetic fields. For instance, cancer rates among electric utility workers with a consistent exposure to electromagnetic fields are on the rise, according to *Delicious!* magazine.[15]

Kryon encourages us to sleep without electric blankets or heated water beds and to even maintain a distance from electric clocks. After discussing this further, he says, "The immunity disease you are now fighting on Earth is magnetically controllable."[16]

Kryon is completely aware of the imminent earth problems but says the population will not be terminated. He urges, "Use the discernment and intuition that is yours at your cellular level. Your higher consciousness *God self* will serve you. Do you think that humankind has been brought to the end of this cycle of higher consciousness enlightenment through entire Earth history to be snuffed by a wave or a boulder?"[17]

He says that many of the prophecies have now been avoided by the manifestation of Love Energy, but he warns that higher vibrations are still needed. Kryon encourages us to continue our meditations and to ask our Angels and Guides for help at all times. There is still great need for many more enlightened ones — Light Workers — willing to help save the planet.

KRYON AT THE U.N.

Two other books have been published since the first one in 1992. As a result, Kryon has become so famous that on November 21, 1995, he was asked to speak at the Society for Enlightenment and Transformation (S.E.A.T.) at the United Nations. He has been only the third channel invited to speak before this meditation group of U.N. dignitaries and workers.[18]

At the U.N., Kryon talked of Love Energy and told the assemblage that there is no negative situation that they cannot change. He said the peace talks in the Middle East, the Berlin walls that tumbled down and the countries who now have once imprisoned political leaders were all due to changes in consciousness.

The only battles on the planet now are what he calls "tribe against tribe," such as in Bosnia and Africa. These negative energies must be settled and then those who are left will "settle themselves" with U.N. help. It was encouraging to note that Kryon did not predict the third world war that many had prophesied.

At the end of his talk he presented four things that he wished the U.N. to focus on:

1. He suggested that scientists working on energy transmission through the ground should slow down, but not stop, or they will cause earthquakes.

2. The diseases ravishing the immune system come from defoliating the planet. Kryon advised there are other diseases in the forest which will remain there only if many will work to keep the biological balance necessary. He implored, "Focus on this in your meditations, and the humans that make the decisions will feel it. Yes, they will!"

3. He urged world leaders to admit to the existence of space visitors and to make public their conversations with them. "Share the news — not in fear, but in enlightenment and in honesty as to what has taken place." Soon their presence will be so widely-known that governments will appear foolish for not having told their people about the extraterrestrials.

4. He asked those assembled to inform metaphysical workers all over the planet about their U.N. room where there is meditation and channeling and feeling the love of Spirit. "Let others know so they can send their love and prayers and give greater power to this important body."

He ended his talk with words of love and "Your personal intent to change yourself can change the reality of the entire planet."

SPECIAL NOTE: *Some highly-respected metaphysical sources have stated that the Kryon books are ninety-percent correct. They consider the other ten percent to be spiritually dangerous. It is recommended that the readers avoid any suggestion for having an implant or getting new Guides. Read closely for any mention of darkness or depression. These are NOT from the Light.*

As with all new material, it is a good idea to pray for protection before reading. There is a plethora of exciting information now available, but ALL of it must be read with discernment. The Angels want us to have a broader understanding of the spirit world and they will protect us from wrong information **IF WE ASK.**

Those searching for answers to avoid earth's destruction have become increasingly aware that the spiritual world is responding to their prayers. It may have gained momentum during a time when there was a tremendous outpouring of prayer, meditation and love during a worldwide event called the Harmonic Convergence in August, 1987. It was an invitation to the spirit world to come and help the earth. What a response! Our *Soul Workers' Group* was told that a billion more Angels had been sent to aid humans in their spiritual efforts and to protect the planet. Beings from distant star systems also answered the call, along with Ascended Masters, Spiritual Guides and spirits such as Kryon that we know little about. An unprecedented number of channeled books, articles, artwork and events took place as the spirit world raced to feed humans new and previously hidden information. This flow of assistance continues.

One of the more vocal extraterrestrial groups was the Pleiadians from the star system Pleiades. They have channeled through many, but trance channel Barbara Marciniak, from North Carolina, received over 400 hours of information. This was condensed into her mind-boggling book, *Bringers of the Dawn.*[19]

The Pleiadians admit to being great story tellers and so the book needs to be read with some skepticism until the channeled information is confirmed by other spiritual sources. They could be telling some parables or they are the best science-fiction authors ever around.

In the book they encourage humans to meditate, work with their intuition and practice discernment, especially when figuring out the different players in the "cosmic ballgame." There are many spirit groups now active on earth and some are negative. Those are referred to by the Pleiadians as the "Dark T-shirts." There are also the "Lizzies," some of whom can be good. Fears sustain the dark entities and they feed off human fears and emotional turmoil. They scheme to spread every bit of bad news throughout the world. The book tells us to notice that most of the media do not seem able to give us much good news. The anger, fear and worry which humans experience after reading or hearing about current problems and violence sustains these dark ones. Not surprisingly, many space visitors encourage humans to not listen to TV or read negative news.

The Pleiadians insist that all emotions are a source of soul nourishment and urge their readers to join with those whose food source is love so the vibrational frequency of the planet can be positively altered.

The biggest revelation from these ETs (and confirmed by Kryon and others) is that our present two-helix DNA will evolve into a twelve-helix molecule. Their story is that about 300,000 years ago, a group of highly-intelligent, but spiritually-low consciousness beings conquered the earth in a Starwars-type of battle. The victors wanted to control the native humans and keep them in their power. Their solution was to rearrange the humans' DNA so their captives would be limited to low intellectual frequencies. They "unplugged" anything not necessary for survival.

The Pleiadians say: "When human DNA begins to rebundle as a twelve-stranded helix, they will have incredible power. Individuals, simply by meeting together and jointly expressing what they want, will be able to change the face of the universe."[20]

Humans choosing to raise their consciousness and bring

Love and Light to the planet are referred to as "the Family of Light." The Pleiadians often mention: "Light is information; ignorance is darkness." Information about the Light we will have and the power and knowledge that the twelve-helix DNA molecule will bring to the planet occupies a formidable part of the book.

Bringers of the Dawn is quite impressive but *You Are Becoming A Galactic Human*,[21] by Virginia Essene and Sheldon Nidle, presents an even broader understanding of current and historical events in earth's existence. This material was channeled from the Sirians, visitors from the Sirius B galaxy.

They claim the historical record of earth covers 35 million years. Our planet has been the focus of interest for quite a few civilizations it seems, with Atlantis considered as "modern times." The Sirians now feel humans could understand the current galactic situations better if we knew our own history.

It appears that the originators of the Star Trek series might have been given extraterrestrial information, since many episodes sound more like fact than science fiction. The Sirians say: there have been numerous Starwars-like battles through the millennia. About four-and-one-half million years ago, the Galactic Federation was formed to keep any attackers in check. Only recently was planet earth allowed to be a member. With our clipped DNA, humans apparently weren't considered bright enough to be a threat to anyone but ourselves. The Sirians confirm the loss of our twelve-helix DNA molecule, but claim it will be restored as humankind goes through an "Ascension" process.

Coming soon is the main event in this process which has been developing for some time. It will occur when our solar system enters a vast region of light called the "photon belt." This will begin with three days of total darkness. There will then begin a restoration of humans to full consciousness and the complete transformation of our DNA and chakra systems.

The Sirians claim: "These unbelievable changes will forever alter not only yourselves, but also your planet and your solar system."[22] At this point, we will all advance from the third to the fifth dimension, with no need to spend time in the fourth dimension.

They also say the photon belt was first discovered by our scientists in 1961. Without a metaphysical understanding, however, they could not grasp the true meaning of their findings. According to the book, the Federation is struggling to prevent some of the major catastrophes predicted for the planet. The end result will be positive, exciting changes for everyone.

There will be mass landings of spaceships before earth enters the photon belt. Everyone willing to listen will be instructed in how to prepare for the dark days when mechanical and electrical devices will be inoperable. All over the planet, Light Workers are being prepared with knowledge of this Ascension process so that they can assist others in their communities and avoid as much panic as possible. It is now almost impossible to go anywhere in the world and not find some who are aware.

Although the information sources vary greatly, the facts seem to coincide in an amazing way. The Angels and extraterrestrials have obviously been working overtime to prepare everyone. Even Hollywood has had a part, with movies like *ET*, *Close Encounters*, *Star Wars* and others. It has prepared us to accept beings from other planets but also to be aware there are still some "Dark T-shirts" lurking around.

Galactic Human is made much more understandable with the inclusion of thirty illustrations scattered throughout the book. The Sirians seem to be a most precise and detailed-oriented group. Or, they just feel that these kindergarten-mentality humans need pictures.

In 1995, Barbara Marciniak wrote her second Pleiadian book called, *Earth — Pleiadian Keys to the Living Library*.[23] In this book, the playful storytellers gave much more information about our planet, but also admitted why they were being so helpful.

They say that eons ago some of their ancestors were allowed to be among the original planners of earth. Highly-evolved civilizations existed here more than a half-million years ago. Remnants of these are buried under the Antarctica ice caps and under layers of sand in the Gobi Desert.

The Pleiadians claim that their ancestors were our ancestors. However, it seems that some of these ancient ones were also those who got power hungry and, being master geneticists, they clipped human DNA. (Aha! So, now they tell us the truth? Maybe...) The Pleiadians confess:

> *It is part of our karma to deal with Earth at this time, for what we set into motion is what we must dance with. Our ancestors created events that presently stifle our development on the Pleiades, and, as Pleiadians, we are seeking to discover solutions to this grand dilemma, a predicament that you share with us. Our civilization, in a future from where you are, is in peril, so we have been impelled to go on a journey to find a solution...*[24]

> *There was a tyranny that was let loose on Earth, and that tyranny has returned to us. Did you know that we made the tyranny, that we stripped you of your heritage of a fully, functioning, twelve-stranded DNA? Do not be naive about Pleiadians, including us. Why do you think we are doing this healing work on your planet? Consider that perhaps we need you for our next phase of development. If*

we wish to grow, we must heal a past that we have been connected to.

Our ancestors have played havoc with your planet as well as assisted you through many, many changes.[25]

After letting us know that their work here is not exactly out of the goodness of their hearts, the Pleiadians proceed to explain many common beliefs about ourselves and earth that we had never realized.

For instance, some of the glorious times that are to follow Earth's upheaval are spelled out. The visitors say that in some areas, vegetation will be grown around meditation, sound and intention as the citizens communicate with nature. People will tone together and make dreams and music together.

The Pleiadians also insist that humans must learn to communicate with plants and animals which receive knowledge directly from the Earth. They have waited many centuries for us to recognize they can help and advise us. They know healing secrets and can feel where the locations are for energy spots. Because humans, as a species, exploit nature, much is hidden from us. Now is the time to start this phase of our education. As we learn to love all things, there will be a cosmic response from nature.

Those willing to awaken and allow the light of knowledge and love to grow within them are in "for a safe and unique adventure into grand arenas of experience."

Those who don't know about extraterrestrial activity are choosing not to pay attention. Even *Time Magazine* (February 5, 1996) quotes sources that say, "Bio-friendly planets may be abundant in the universe." On page 58, we read, "...in a sense, the search for ET life is really a search for ourselves... who we are and what our place is in the grand sweep of the cosmos."

Sounds like what the Pleiadians told us.

Each step in the journey toward "enlightenment" is exciting but almost too much at times for our simple minds to comprehend. Every week we hear new information. For instance, one source tells about the underground cities which have been on earth since a need to hide arose many centuries ago. Who are these people? Are they human like us? Is this true at all?

I finally decided to check things out with my own wonderful guide and friend, Simon. With my husband, Robert, we prayed and then asked Simon to visit and give us some guidance. Within moments of my going into deep relaxation, he spoke through me with his usual cheery greeting. After exchanging pleasantries, Robert asked some detailed questions.

Robert: What do you think about all the Earth Changes, the underground people, the Pleiadians, the Sirians and everything we're hearing and reading?

SIMON: Oh, my, such a compound, complex question. Well, I'll do my best to help you understand better. It hasn't always sunk in with the Light Workers, but I have said many times that there are things happening on MANY dimensions. You do not see them, so it is hard for you to believe in them. Even being in the Spirit world, we do not always know what is going on because there are dimensions that even we are not aware of. You know, we each have our own job. We can't run around and keep track of everything. We leave that to God. We do what it is we are supposed to do and work within the elements and dimensions where we belong. So, while I can find out many things if it is important to do so, we just try to help humans stay in their here and now time. We are happy if they can just handle that well.

I can tell you, however, that it is true that humans will be coming up to the fifth dimension. Not just the fourth, mind you, but the fifth. It will be a spectacular shift of consciousness. When is the exact time this will happen? It is unfortunate that someone is always predicting, "Oh, it will happen on this month or this year on this day."

You must realize that in our world and on other dimensions, there is no space and time as you know it. So, we are not compelled to do something according to your schedule. You see?

Well, these predictions sell books, don't they?

Of course. And they are not all garbage. There is a tremendous amount of information that is being sent to earth now. This happens as people allow themselves to be open to Spirit and become channels as Joy has. But predictions are tricky.

As in my case, we DO NOT know everything and it is very difficult to answer people who want to know "Exactly when?" You cannot begin to imagine what a huge undertaking is going on. It is as if you have a gigantic picture puzzle with over a thousand pieces and you must put each one in the correct place or it isn't right. Or, think in terms of wiring a whole city... a big one. Say you have this new city — not just one house but a whole city — and you want to turn on all the lights at one time. Well, obviously, you need many, many people going about doing different jobs. It would never get done with just one person, right? So, there is preparation as if it were Christmas time and all the lights needed to go at once to get this great effect.

It's a remarkable event! But it has taken the work of many and it must all be coordinated. And this is where problems can develop because all the coordinates don't always work the way they are supposed to. Also, to do the "publicity," we must deal with humans who don't always perform the way we would like either. They have free will and, even when we aren't dealing with humans, we must work with free will.

The whole spirit world is trying very hard to get everyone to daily work on raising their consciousness so they can be a Light to others. No one can do it by just sitting there and watching their boob tube. Even those sitting in a small room can do their part by sending out Light and Love to others. It needn't be a large job that a person is doing, but every small part is essential. Humans have trouble believing the great power they have when they send out these loving vibrations. This Light and Love needs to bombard every inch of the planet to bring up the vibrations. It takes the work of many.

You have to ask yourself, "Am I fulfilling my assignment here? Am I helping to put all these little switches together for a particular house so that, in the end, the whole city can light up at once?" From those of you who know about these things, much is expected. It is very scriptural you know. "To whom much has been given, much is expected."

I'm not putting any guilt on you or on anyone else. I'm simply saying, this is the message you must give to yourself and to others in order to make things happen with as little pain as possible. Unfortunately, pain makes mankind think and it is often a necessary way to get attention. If you can get things in order without pain, you must agree that it is much better.

There has just been this gigantic hurricane in your coastal region which was very, very devastating. It tore apart certain areas where there was darkness and negativity. In other words, if enough people had gotten together, they could have prayed the storm apart and it would have had no force whatsoever. Get a group to send Love and Light into the eye of the next hurricane you hear about and see what happens.

Do you understand what I am saying to you? You have tremendous power when you work with Holy Spirit. Of yourself you do nothing, but with God, ALL things are possible. It is so human to be lackadaisical about what seems to be going on. "Well, is this going to happen or not?" "When are events to occur?" "Do I need to worry or can I just sit here and do what I want to?" SUCH QUESTIONS! Yes, do something while you can. There isn't much time left. There are a lot of things afoot. You are a part of what will happen whether you want to be or not. So, start helping to get this city wired right!

You asked if there were underground cities. Yes, there are and not just on earth. Because there are many things underground on other planets, your best telescopes cannot usually see them. Groups are coming from these cities, too.

There are many different extraterrestrials here. They may be more evolved than Earth humans, but not so evolved that ego doesn't sometime get in the way. And jealousy. One group says, "We're here to save the world with our mighty power." Then other groups reply, "Hah! The heck you are. We're here to do that." This is why you have been encouraged to pray for ALL the spirit world. Even Guides and Angels enjoy receiving Love and Light, you know. It does help us.

Now, understand that the Angels have been given charge of the Earth project and they just keep on working in spite of bickering by "the help." They don't pay too much attention because, fortunately, they work with unconditional Love and without ego. So, you see, with all these groups there are billions of souls because this is going to be a BIG event. I mean, this is bigger than anything you could possibly imagine. So, you should be most pleased that you have been invited to take part in all this.

If you had gotten an invitation from the President, would you not consider it a very special occasion? Yes? Certainly, you would. Well, this is a much more important invitation than if you were invited to have dinner with the President. Because you are living in your third dimension and cannot see, or even sometimes believe, what this is all about, it is difficult to "get with the program" as you say.

This is why sometimes things have to be done to get your attention. If the Weather Angels had a hurricane come zipping through *your living room, it would get your attention, would it not? Well?*

Yes, certainly, but I don't know if we get the message. Do you think that the hurricane that just came through conveyed a message?

It was supposed to. That's what these things are all about. It's what all of these happenings are about.

When talking about the ETs, you mentioned their egos. Is the ego present in the fourth and fifth dimensions?

If you read A Course In Miracles *you know that the ego is really a non-entity which you can create because you have free will. The only real thing is Spirit. Holy Spirit will answer your questions and work with you — if you choose that direction. If you choose to make your own fantasy world and create an ego then, of course, it exists as far as you are concerned. In reality, there is no such thing.*

The ETs are way beyond the third dimension but still struggle with various stages of development, some of them good, some of them not so good. Even though they should know better, at times they compare themselves to humans and feel, "Well, we're just so great."

They forget that this is all about bringing together all of human-kind and not just Earth humans. Everyone is to come together because we are all this spark of consciousness in the mind of God and we must go back as one. We will not, CANNOT, go back individually, you see, and this is why your assignment, and everyone else's, is vital and essential.

In other words, "To thine ownself be true."

Exactly. You must always work at really understanding yourself and who you are. This is not an easy task. Humans seem to try all their lives to know themselves and then they usually don't succeed too well.

It may be even harder now with everything so speeded up. This is why you have been given A Course In Miracles *and other works: to bring all these psychological and theological understandings together so that you have some help. When science and spirituality are brought together, you will learn much quicker.*

You have also been given leisure time so that you can concentrate on improving yourself and learn how powerful your mind can be. Unfortunately, what does humankind do? They waste most of their free time or busy themselves with useless tasks. Back in my time, a few hundred years ago, the ordinary peasants had no leisure time at all. They were expected to work many long, long hours and got a few hours off on Sunday to go to Church. And, except for special occasions, that was usually all they got. Although I was from the so-called "leisure class," I still had my work of looking after things. I could, however, read and travel so that my learning and understanding were far beyond the average person's.

Today, many of your fellow travelers on the earth plane are given much leisure time so they can grow. And this is what it has been given for. Instead, what is this time usually used for? It is frittered away for the most part. We must work with those who are willing to accept their role as Light Workers and teachers; to help all of us become one in God. I know you have heard about those who will just have to be lifted off and taken to another less-evolved planet. Their refusal to hear and grow means that there is no way they can be a part of the tremendous growth that this planet is now ready to experience. Yes, it will bring what is called "the thousand years of peace." No one knows how long it will actually be since there is always free will.

Mother Earth must heal herself and, with the new consciousness, everyone will understand she is a living entity, a part of this whole venture. There is a great deal of healing that must be done. Is this going to be completed before the millennium? I can't tell you. Maybe it will. Maybe it won't. There are so many things that have to be put into place and so these people, who have been working and worrying so much about the Earth Changes, and all the things that are to happen, may be really disappointed if not much is happening. It's simply that they are all hung up on this linear time business and that's not where it's at. It's in growing, in helping, in giving of yourself in one form or another.

The big thing is to convince people about what is happening; and that IT IS going to happen.

Yes. You sort of indicated that's why you called me here. Your first task is to convince yourself. You are not one-hundred percent sure yourself, are you?

I read a lot of conflicting things.

Well, you may read some conflicting things, but basically, it is fairly simple. The consciousness of those who are open is being brought up quicker and quicker. Time is speeding up very fast — your linear time, that is. And there is a cast of billions weaving things together so that everything can be made ready for what we call the Ascension Process. It is all happening. Be a part of these exciting times!

Is this quickening the reason we feel we never have enough time to do things?

Of course. There's so much to do and not enough time. Hustle, hustle, hustle all the time because we're speeding so rapidly. There is no doubt about that. In a sense you have less time every day because you don't recognize that the Angels are quite capable of slowing down time or speeding it up. They can do either one for you and so, if you need more time, ask for it. Surprised, yes?

Oh, my dear sir, you can do so much and you have not begun to explore the vastness of your own mind. I repeat: You have not begun to explore the vastness of your own mind. It is capable of so much and *you are still in the kindergarten stage, you might say. This is no insult to you at all, or meant that way. It is simply to help you realize that there is so much excitement going on that you can be a part of.*

I feel like I'm in kindergarten sometimes.

I know and many share your feeling. Joy said she was delighted that her Soul Workers' Group got promoted to first grade and probably to second grade. They did make great, great progress and they worked very hard at it and they continue to work very hard. Sometimes, they still get quite confused. Don't feel that you are the only one who gets confused. Continue to pray and meditate and ask and it will become clearer. Can you imagine what graduate school is like?

And now, I am being called. Is there anything more?

Thank you. You have answered a lot of our questions. Thank you for coming.

You are quite welcome. And so, goodbye for now and God's blessings be on both of you.

Dr. Joy: And so, we continue to work, pray and learn. Graduate school? Oh, my!

CHAPTER 12

Saving The World — & Ourselves

*S*aving *the world and ourselves* is the same thing. There is only one way and it sounds easy, but it's probably the hardest thing to accomplish. "It" is simply "unconditional love." How do you do that? You can't. You must allow it to happen to you and "It" happens only in THE Silence. Or, as St. Augustine advised, "Return into yourself."

To save the world, wouldn't we climb high mountains or do great tasks? But to be quiet so quiet that we can hear God talk to us, and to do it EVERY day! We're just too busy. We have things to do and places to go. Sure, we want to grow in love. Just give us a self-help book to read or a cassette to listen to while we're driving and that would be great. But to sit… just sit and do nothing? That's difficult if not impossible. And yet, from ancient mystics to modern spiritual teachers and channels, the message is the same. We must enter THE Silence. We are told over and over that all the answers are within.

THE Silence must be understood as being different from just a quiet time while we are doing tasks and our thoughts are roaming to other things. When in THE Silence, nothing else is being done and a sincere effort is made to gently dismiss any busy thoughts that might enter the mind. It can actually be described as going to "a place within us." It is in this place that we can "hear" God. Actually, we hear His messengers.

If we have prayerfully asked for Divine Guidance, what we receive may be from our Guardian Angel or from Jesus or from some other spiritual figure. It is good to ask who the words are from if we are not yet familiar with our Spiritual Guide. Sometimes messages are in words, other times just through an inner knowing. THE Silence is a place without words, a place where everything we need to know is just simply understood.

The spiritual world is not hampered by language. The Angels "vibrate" or "tone" their thoughts. Some people feel this. Others say, "I don't know how to explain it because there were no words, but I just KNEW what I was to understand." Frequently, they have asked a question and this is how it was answered.

"I sat there for fifteen minutes and didn't learn a thing," some will say. THE Silence usually takes time to develop. Meditation is a discipline that most have to work at for a while. When results happen, that is nice. But results are not the purpose. The purpose is to open self to Universal Love; to practice FEELING oneness with God and to give out what love we have to the world and all that is in the world.

When we can visualize our loved ones and the whole planet surrounded by the brilliant Light of God's love, we may experience a beautiful inner peace. A few have experienced inner "fireworks." This has frightened some and they were afraid to meditate again for a long time. This was especially true if they had a sensation of being lifted up out of their bodies and into a sparkling spiritual realm. This seldom happens, however, and should not be the purpose of the person praying. Practice patiently and understanding will eventually follow.

> *Listen for the whisper in your heart. You will hear it when your thoughts are still. Focus upon it until it fills your being and becomes the motivational energy behind all your actions.*
> – The *Starseed Transmissions* (Page 78)

Some of our great modern mystics have given us insightful words to help us grow. For instance, **Thomas Merton**, a Trappist monk, wrote:

> *In solitude I have at last discovered that You have desired the love of my heart, O my God, the love of my heart as it is — the love of a man's heart.*
>
> *...Only solitude has taught me that I do not have to be a god or an angel to be pleasing to You, that I do not have to become a pure intelligence without feeling and without human imperfection before You will listen to my voice.*
>
> *...this is the mystery of our vocation: not that we cease to be men in order to become angels or gods, but that the love of my man's heart can become God's love for God and men, and my human tears can fall from my eyes as the tears of God because they well up from the motion of His Spirit in the heart of His incarnate Son. Hence, the Gift of Piety grows in solitude, nourished by the Psalms.*
>
> *When this is learned, then our love of other men becomes pure and strong. We can go out to them without vanity and without complacency, loving them with something of the purity and gentleness and hiddenness of God's love for us.*
>
> *This is the true fruit and the true purpose of Christian solitude.*[1]

While meditation is often considered to come from Eastern faiths, it is prominent in ancient Christianity and Judaism. The difficulties and the rewards are often very similar when writers of Eastern and Western religions report their experiences.

Their "prayer time" will have some differences, because God didn't give any rules about it. But, Christian monks and laity, Zen Buddhists, Transcendental Meditation devotees and others all seem to reach the same understanding. THE Silence is what one should be striving to attain. Within this Silence, we can descend into ourselves and into Total Love.

Here are some words from **J. Krishnamurti,** an Eastern teacher of international fame.

> *In the life we generally lead there is very little solitude. Even when we are alone our lives are crowded by so many influences, so much knowledge, so many memories of so many experiences, so much anxiety, misery and conflict that our minds become duller and duller, more and more insensitive, functioning in a monotonous routine.*

> *...We carry our burdens all the time. We never die to them. We never leave them behind. It is only when we give complete attention to a problem and solve it immediately — never carrying it over to the next day, the next minute — that there is solitude. Then, even if we live in a crowded house or are in a bus, we have solitude. And that solitude indicates a fresh mind, an innocent mind.*

> *To have inward solitude and space is very important because it implies freedom to be, to go, to function, to fly. After all, goodness can only flower in space just as virtue can flower only when there is freedom.*

One can see directly that it is only when the mind is silent that there is a possibility of clarity. The whole purpose of meditation in the East is to bring about such a state of mind: that is, to control thought.[2]

Krishnamurti emphasizes that we need to learn to control our thoughts. When we succeed in stilling our minds, we can accomplish much more. Eventually we find it possible to bring this inner peace into our everyday world.

While pondering the difficulties for modern people to succeed in attaining this wondrous state, my sister Gloria called me from her home in Arlington, Virginia. She had just come back from a two-week wilderness canoe and camping trip. With five other women, they had taken three canoes into a pristine and isolated park area in Ontario, north of Minnesota. I was concerned about the cold and rain and I had heard about flies and mosquitoes that were bigger than baseballs. So, my first question to her was: "Would you go again?"

"In a heartbeat!" she assured me. "It was wonderful!"

Fortunately, they had warm weather and only one rainy day, so I began to see the possibilities for a good vacation.

"The birds, the trees, the mists, the sounds of the water and the magnificent Silence," she enthused.

(Ah, Silence. The Angels had more for me to learn.)

My sister's group understood that Silence was important and planned on two hours a day when they would not speak. One day they spent five hours in Silence. For six women, together for two weeks and in such close proximity, I considered this an amazing feat.

Gloria said, "One day we got up about 4 a.m., so we could break camp and paddle into the sunrise in Silence. What an incredible experience! I just can't explain it in words."

She continued, "The beauty of just being quiet helps you to go deeper and deeper inside yourself and feel the oneness with others and nature. You begin to feel the rhythms of the earth as you slow yourself down."

I was curious to know how six women managed to get along for two weeks in a wilderness area without all the "civilized" trappings to which we have become accustomed, especially warm showers and indoor plumbing.

"It was amazing," answered Gloria. "There was some adjustment at first; but as we progressed down the river and became enveloped by Nature, the beauty and the Silence, we had an internal shift. We became one with the rhythmic strokes of the paddle and the whole Universe. Sharing experiences that couldn't be explained gave us a feeling of interconnectedness with God, nature and each other. We became more open, more aware, more alive. It was like growing in love.

"We were able to FEEL at a deeper level; like having our hearts opened. Even the loons must have felt it for they let us come very close to them. Folklore claims this is supposed to be a sign of blessing from this ancient and fragile bird.

"The mystics write about experiencing this cosmic love all day and I think this must have been what they were talking about. The whole trip seemed like a meditation and now I really know what a walking meditation is."

"And after returning home?" I asked. She paused thoughtfully and said, "I feel like I'm drawing from a deeper well. It has helped me to be more centered, more rooted. And, yes, more alive!"

So, it IS possible to know THE Silence in big doses today.

Silence brings peace and strength as well as an awakening of our perception to a greater reality. Two-week wilderness trips may be out for most of us, but we can eventually obtain similar results with daily quiet times.

"Let there be peace and let it begin with me," shows us that this is truly a way to help save the world. Our inner peace has to result in a greater love for everyone and everything. In Annie Kirkwood's second book of Mother Mary's messages, *Mary's Message of Hope*, the Mother of Jesus tells us again how unbelievably powerful LOVE is. Real Divine love, that is. She says it is more powerful than atomic energy! A staggering thought, but one that makes us aware that this is something we must know about. But, how do we get to that point? Well, in THE Silence, of course.

In answering a question about how we are to help the world, **Mary, the Mother of Jesus,** gave this answer:

> *By staying true to your inner search. By keeping your connection to the Father, Creator. This is so important, my children. How can you light the way if your lamp is dimmed? How can you guide if you know not the way? How can you be prepared to serve, if you know not how to prepare?*
>
> *This is the commitment I request, that each of you increase your prayer time, increase your earnest desire to know. Let sincerity be the byword for your inner search. You cannot depend on anyone else. Do not seek to find your answers, or connection, through any church official, guru or anyone who is a creation of the Father.*
>
> *I see many seeking to take a shortcut in the process.*

They seek to find the way through different exercises in meditation and through differing theories. Guided meditations are good, but not when they are used exclusively. The purpose of meditation is to receive. How can the Father speak to your inner mind and heart if it is cluttered? Silence is important. Silence is the way the Father speaks to you, because of your fear. It is not the only way He can speak to you.

God, the Father, is so very loving, gentle and compassionate. He knows that race consciousness is very steeped in fear. Even when you have eliminated it as best you can, there is residue. So be committed to meditating in silence at least once a day. Let the Father guide you. Allow the Father to work through you. Your truth can come only through you. The truth, as it applies to your life and the circumstances in your life, can only come through you. Trust your inner awareness. If it is not clear to you, then ask for clarity. Ask for definition.

Understand that as the representative of the Divine Maternal Energy, I am available to all people. I will come to you with angels and with the Love of God. Let your prayers be to the Father, but I am ever ready to help you connect to the Father.

Angels await only the word; they will help if you prefer. Know deep within, you are loved! You are already accepted in your present form. You are already in the presence of God, already filled with His light and love. Recognize that. You know all you need to know. It will come to you as you choose to follow Spirit's guidance. My request, then, is for you to seek within for the Father. Support each other and pray for each other.

Now my dear children, live in peace. Remember that Love is a very powerful energy, more powerful than atomic energy. I have faith in your abilities to heed my words. I appreciate your efforts and attention.

Understand, dear ones, the Father hears your every thought. Speak to Him in your mind. Let Him be the one who helps with every endeavor. Healings will come from your prayers. Simply allow the process to work. Remain in peace and love. I am loving you. The Father loves all of us even more.[3]

Mary's message is stronger as she warns of soon-to-come turmoil and the world-shaking earthquake that leaves us in total darkness for three days. Her gentle encouragement to learn answers while in THE Silence is not new but an important reminder.

Translated from ancient writings, this section from a classic spiritual book, **Light On The Path,** explains the unfolding of the soul as it soars toward God:

Look for the flower to bloom in the silence that follows the storm: not till then. It shall grow, it will shoot up. It will make branches and leaves and form buds, while the storm continues, while the battle lasts. But not till the whole personality is dissolved and melted — not until it is held by the Divine fragment which has created it — not until the whole of nature has yielded and become subject unto its higher self, can the bloom open. Then will come a calm such as comes in a tropical country after the heavy rain, when Nature works so swiftly that one may see her action. Such a calm will come to the harassed spirit. And in the deep Silence the mysterious event will occur which will prove that the way has been found.

Call it by what name you will; it is a voice that speaks where there is none to speak. It is a messenger that comes, a messenger without form or substance, or it is the flower of the soul that has opened. It cannot be described by any metaphor. But it can be felt after, looked for, and desired even amid the raging of the storm. The Silence may last a moment of time or it may last a thousand years. But it will end. Yet you will carry its strength with you. Again and again the battle must be fought and won. It is only for an interval that Nature can be still.[4]

From **Matthew Fox** we read in The Coming of the Cosmic Christ:

...the mystic is also a befriender of silence. Returning to the source of one's being is rarely an experience that can be expressed in words. Kabir says "Anyone who has had a taste of this love is so enchanted that he is stricken with silence."

Have you ever been "stricken with silence?" If so you have tasted the ineffable; you have had a mystical experience. Silence is too often defined as "the absence of something" when it is much more than that. Silence is also a search for something, a search for the depths for the source. Many of the mystical awakenings experienced by astronauts and cosmonauts in space have been triggered by the cosmic silence they have encountered there.

Similar things happen to persons swimming in the depths of the sea or spelunking in the caves of Mother Earth. Silence moves people. That is why it is so essential to meditation practices, including the art of listening to our images. Being, one might say, is silent. We must embrace silence in order to experience being. Then — and only then — does it speak deep truths to us.

...The mystic in us yearns for silent time and for our letting go of images.[5]

"How do I know I'm not hearing what's in my own mind?" is often heard from those starting on a spiritual path. In the beginning, that's exactly what you do hear, your own voice. For many, it might be best to start by playing a guided meditation on a cassette player. There are many available from book and music stores. Eventually, you will be able to discard these except on days when your mind is spinning and you need some help in slowing your thoughts down.

Remember, the purpose is to relax your mind and let God's ideas in. Even though you cannot stop your thoughts, God is able to sprinkle his messages in between them like stardust falling from heaven, When distracting thoughts come, and they will, gently push them away. Don't get upset about them or feel you are a failure. Your job is to set some time apart for God and make an honest effort. Let Him do the rest.

We all have some spiritual gifts. Those who are "clairaudient" can internally hear spiritual voices. They can actually learn to have a dialogue with their Angel, Guide or Holy Spirit. With practice, it is as if you were hearing your best friend on the phone. You recognize the voice(s) and the words are loving and encouraging, sometimes humorous. For those who do not yet recognize the spiritual voices, pray before starting a meditation in order to silence the sound of any but these. If there are earthbound or dark side attachments, they may try to get your attention. Pray for the Light; it always overcomes darkness.

Others do not hear, but they are strongly intuitive and will KNOW and understand without words. They may find this confusing at first but will, eventually, learn to accept their gift.

Others may be "clairvoyant" and mentally see clear pictures or happenings. Finally, there are those who just FEEL things. They will walk into a room and feel what kind of energies are there; possibly what kind of temperament the people who live there have. They also, just KNOW.

All of these are valid means of communication from God and may be considered part of the sixth sense. Strive to develop your own gift(s). A few have all of the gifts. They need to work very hard at staying grounded as they may not be the most practical people around for everyday matters.

Heavenly language was explained in great detail in 1758 by the amazing **Emmanuel Swedenborg**, scientist and clairvoyant. Here are a few passages conveying his understanding of heavenly communication:

> 236. *There is a single language for everyone in all heaven. They all understand each other, no matter what community they come from, near or far. The language is not learned there; it is native to everyone. It actually flows from their affection and thought.*

> 248. *The speech of angels or spirits with man sounds*

just as "audible" as the speech of one person with another.
However, it is not audible to people nearby, only to the
individual himself. This is because the speech of an angel or
spirit flows into the person's thought first, and comes by an
inner path to his physical ear; it thus activates it from within.
But the speech of one person with another travels through
the air first, comes by an outer path to his physical ear, and
activates it from the outside.

...In evidence of this descent from within of an angel's
or spirit's speech, I have observed that it also travels to the
tongue and makes it quiver slightly, though not with the kind
of motion that occurs when the person himself is using his
tongue to enunciate speech sounds.[6]

While Spirits usually wait for us to communicate with
them, that is not always the case. For some, there is a physical
vibration that indicates that their Spirit Guide or Angel has a
message for them or for someone accompanying them.

For instance, Balbir becomes aware that a message is to
come through him when he feels his tongue start to quiver. He
finds this embarrassing, especially when he is in the middle of
a conversation. I have seen him put his hand over his mouth to
cover it. Then he gets up and walks away as it is almost
impossible for him to talk. If he is at home, he goes to his
"meditation room" and begins to pray. If the message is for
someone else, he motions for the person to follow him. After a
short time, he is quiet and the information pours out of him in
an avalanche of words.

How to start meditating is an individual process. There are
several suggestions, such as: Do it on an empty stomach. After

eating, it is difficult to stay awake and you may end up with a snooze instead of a meditation.

Next, find a quiet place. "In my house?" you ask. "It's always noisy there."

Find a large closet, or even go into a bathroom where you can close the door and mentally still your mind. Go wherever it is you need to be so that you can leave the chaos behind. This, by itself, will do wonders for you physically as well as spiritually and emotionally.

If you can get away from the house, drive to a park or some other place where it is quiet. Naturally, it is nice if you can go to a chapel or have a special "meditation room" like Balbir has, but that may not be practical. However, in channeling, the Angels have suggested we set apart a small corner in our house where we go to meditate. Put up a small table, or even a TV tray, and put a cloth on it. Treat it as an altar. You might have flowers, a candle and a holy picture or statue. Your tape recorder could be on or near the table so that you can play relaxing, meditative music. There should be a straight chair or cushion for you to sit upon. After meditating here a few times, your subconscious will automatically start to relax you when you come to this quiet spot. The space can be as small as three feet by three feet. It can and should be quite simple.

If you cannot close your eyes and keep your mind from wandering, you may want to light a candle and focus your attention on it. Concentrate and repeat to yourself something like "God's Light is the Light of the world within us." Similar thoughts can then be concentrated on. God will put His thoughts into yours no matter how you choose to reach Him. White Eagle tells us: "Within the Silence one touches the heart of God."

Most of the world sits on the floor in yoga fashion to meditate, but Westerners are more comfortable in chairs. If seats are for you, that's fine, but it is important to have a straight backed seat rather than a soft, cushiony couch or chair. Keeping your backbone straight will allow energies to flow gently up your spine and help you keep your mind alert. A wooden prayer seat may work for you or you may prefer to kneel to pray.

Whatever method you choose for meditation, remember that if your body becomes uncomfortable, your mind will begin to wander and you will lose focus. Always maintain your comfort. You will be less distracted.

Starting meditation with prayer makes our intentions known to God and our Spirit Guides. All healing begins with gratitude and a prayer of thanksgiving is a good way to start healing the earth and all that is in it. Acknowledge first that God IS Love. This is how we connect with our Creator, our Source.

Remember that our Angels love us, too. They are delighted to assist us if we ask for their help. Thank them for being our constant companions, helpers and spiritual guides. Ask them to "Take us into THE Silence that we may 'hear;' that we may know God's truth and His will for us."

You may find it helpful to do some spiritual reading before you begin meditation. This quiets and focuses your thoughts. Then, pray to God as you would speak to a close friend.

Begin serious contemplation by taking slow, deep breaths. This cleanses your body of toxins and stills your mind. Breathe in peace and breathe out any concerns or worries that are bothering you. Your Spirit Guides cannot reach you until you release all of your problems to them. Worry, depression and discouragement are not from God — peace, tranquility and love are.

Four deep breaths are often enough to relax yourself, especially if you concentrate on different parts of your body. For instance, deep breath one: feel (or sense) all the muscles in your legs and feet relax; deep breath two: send the oxygen, across the back of your neck and down your arms until you feel everything go limp; deep breath three: pull a golden white Light down into the top of your head and feel your eyes and facial muscles become relaxed; deep breath four: feel the oxygen flowing through your body and your stomach and all your organs loosen up. Soon you will be able to totally relax your whole body by just counting up to four as you take deep breaths. It's a great stress management technique.

Sometimes a short affirmation, repeated at each inhalation or exhalation is helpful. I often repeat; "The Father and I are one," or "Jesus loves me." At this point, some recommend that, as you relax, you let a gentle smile form on your face. This is a physical expression of the total joy that comes through communion with the Beloved.

From this point, be content to be in His Holy Presence. Do NOTHING. Say NOTHING. You have taken out the "trash" from your minds. Let God fill you as He will. In this simplicity, be receptive. If you receive only a quiet, clear mind, that is God's blessing to you. If Spirit needs you to know something, you will know it. Perhaps there is nothing you need to know at this moment. God may choose to fill you with a little more Love. Be grateful for this gift. It is more precious to you than all the world's gold.

❖ ❖ ❖

And finally, from the text of **A Course In Miracles,** we read:

There is a place in you where this whole world
has been forgotten; where no memory
of sin and of illusion lingers still.
There is a place in you which time has left,
and echoes of eternity are heard.
There is a resting place so still no sound
except a hymn to Heaven rises up
to gladden God the Father and the Son.
Where Both abide are They remembered, Both.
And where They are is Heaven and is peace.

Think not that you can change Their dwelling place
For your Identity abides in Them,
and where They are, forever must you be.
The changelessness of Heaven is in you,
so deep within that nothing in this world
but passes by, unnoticed and unseen.
The still infinity of endless peace
surrounds you gently in its soft embrace,
so strong and quiet,
tranquil in the might of
its Creator, nothing can
intrude upon the sacred
Son of God within.[7]

Epilogue

And so we say, "Amen" and pray
that we meet one another on our
high journey of Spiritual flight.
We pray, too, that we are all filled
with gifts from our Creator.
Love. Peace. Joy.
These are gifts only
our Creator can give us.

Love and Blessings from:
Joy, Simon, Angels & Guides

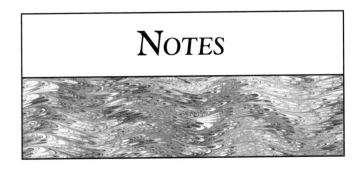

NOTES

*Chapter 1: Ghosts, Attachments & Things
That Go Bump In The Night*

1. Dr. William J. Baldwin, D.D.S., Ph.D., *Spirit Releasement Therapy: A Technique Manual* (Falls Church, VA: The Human Potential Foundation Press, 1993).

2. Dr. Edith Fiore, *The Unquiet Dead... a Psychologist Treats Spirit Possession* (New York: Ballantine Books, 1988).

3. *Ghosts* (A Paramount Film, 1990).

4. George W. Meek, *After We Die, What Then?* (Columbus, OH: Ariel Press, 1987).

5. *The Old Testament*, Samuel, 16:23.

6. Carl A. Wickland, M.D., *30 Years Among The Dead* (U.S.A.: Newcastle Publishing Co., Inc., 1974).

7. Ibid., p. 28.

8. Ibid., p. 16.

9. Ibid., p. 34.

10. Ibid., p. 17.

11. Ibid., p. 23.

12. Ibid., p. 311

13. Ibid., p. 389.

14. Ibid., back of title page.

15. Ibid., p. 19.

Chapter 3: I Talk To The Devil — It's A Cold Day In Hell

1. Oakland Press, *We Ignore Signs of Satanism, Experts Say* (Pontiac, MI; October 1993).

2. Michelle Smith and Lawrence Pazder, M.D., *Michelle Remembers* (New York, NY, Pocket Books, a Simon & Schuster division of Gulf & Western Corporation, 1980).

3. Ibid., p. 25.

4. Scripps Howard (*America Faces 'Ticking Time Bomb' in growing youth*).

5. Jack Jones (Gannett News Service).

6. William J. Baldwin, D.D.S., Ph.D., *Spirit Releasement Therapy: A Technique Manual* (The Human Potential Foundation Press, 1993).

Chapter 4: Nature Spirits Collaborate With Humans

1. The Findhorn Community, *The Findhorn Garden* (New York: Harper & Row, Publishers, 1975), pp. 8-9

2. Paul Hawken, *The Magic of Findhorn* (New York, New York: Bantam Book, 1975), p. 46.

3. Ibid., p. 57-58.

4. Cindy McGonagle, *Angel Times* (Atlanta, GA: Angelic Realms Unlimited, Inc., 1995), Volume 1, Issue 3, pp. 14, 38.

5. Geoffrey Hodson, *The Brotherhood of Angels and Men* (Wheaton, IL: Theosophical Publishing House, 1982), p. 1.

6. Geoffrey Hodson, *Fairies at Work and at Play* (Wheaton, IL: Theosophical Publishing House, 1982), pp. 58-59.

7. Molly Sheehan, *Green Hope Farm Newsletter* (Meriden, NH, Fall, 1995), pp. 1-3.

8. Edward Bach, M.D., *Heal Thyself* in *The Bach Flower Remedies* (New Canaan, CT: Keats Publishing Company, 1979).

9. Joyce Petrak, *How To Remember Bach Flower Remedies or... First, Get The Elephant Off Your Foot* (Lenoir City, TN: Curry-Peterson Press, 1991).

10. Molly Sheehan, *Flower Essences — A Guide to Green Hope Farm* (Meriden, NH, 1994).

11. Rev. Franklin Loehr, *The Power of Prayer on Plants* (New York, NY: The New American Library, Inc., 1969).

12. Peter Tompkins and Christopher Bird, *The Secret Life of Plants* (New York, NY: Avon Books, 1974), p. xv.

13. Larry Dossey, M.D., *Healing Words* (New York, NY: Harper Collins Publishers, 1940).

Chapter 8: Soul Rescue In Vietnam

1. Daniel, Wyllie & Ramer, *Ask Your Angel* (Ballantine Books, 1992).

Chapter 9: Different Methods & Protection

1. Eugene Maurey, *Exorcism* (Whitford Press, 1988).

2. Ibid., p. 119.

3. Aloa Starr, *Prisoners of Earth* (Light Technology, 1993).

4. Ibid., p. 99.

5. Carole Sanborn Langlois, *Soul Rescue — Help on the Way Home to Spirit* (That's the Spirit Publishing Company, 1993).

6. Ibid., p. 20.

7. Ibid., p. 249.

8. Dr. Edith Fiore, *The Unquiet Dead* (Ballantine books, 1988), p. 138.

9. Irene Hickman, D.O., *Remote Depossession* (Hickman Systems, 1994), p. 14.

Chapter 10: Dolphins, Whales & The Environment

1. Gary Kowalski, *The Souls of Animals* (Walpol, NH: Stillpoint Publishing, 1991), p. 110-111.

2. *Center of Attention* (Santa Clara, CA: Issue 4, February 8, 1995).

3. John Muir, *An Adventure With A Dog and A Glacier* (Century Magazine, September, 1897).

4. Associated Press, *World Religious Leaders Plan New Activism on Environment* (July 3, 1996).

Chapter 11: Are These The End Times?

1. White Eagle, *Spiritual Unfoldment 2* (Hampshire, England: The White Eagle Publishing Trust, 1969).

2. *A Course In Miracles* (Mill Valley, CA: Foundation for Inner Peace, 1976).

3. Robert Skutch, *Journey Without Distance* (Berkeley: CA: Celestial Arts, 1984).

4. Annie Kirkwood, *Mary's Message To The World* (Nevada City, CA: Blue Dolphin Press, 1991).

5. Ibid., Chapter 4.

6. Ibid., p. 71.

7. Ibid., title page.

8. Sun Bear with Wabun Wind, *Black Dawn, Bright Day* (New York, NY: Fireside, 1992).

9. Ibid., p. 189.

10. Ibid., p. 28.

11. Ibid., p. 25.

12. Lee Carroll, *Kryon, The End Times* (Del Mar, CA: The Kryon Writings, 1995).

13. Ibid., p. 11.

14. Ibid., p. 13.

15. *Delicious! Magazine*

16. Carroll, *Kryon, The End Times*, p. 20.

17. Ibid., p. 22.

18. Lee Carroll, *Connecting Link Magazine*, Issue 32 (Alto, MI: E.L.I., 1996), p. 21.

19. Barbara Marciniak, *Bringers of the Dawn* (Santa Fe, NM: Bear & Company Publishing Co., 1992).

20. Ibid., p. 20.

21. Virginia Essene and Sheldon Nidle, *You Are Becoming A Galactic Human* (Santa Clara, CA: Spiritual Education Endeavors, 1994).

22. Ibid., p. 27.

23. Barbara Marciniak, *Earth* (Santa Fe, NM: Bear & Company, Inc., 1995).

24. Ibid., p. 3.

25. Ibid., p. 13.

Chapter 12: Saving The World — And Ourselves

1. Thomas Merton, *Thoughts in Solitude* (Garden City, New York: A Doubleday Image Book, 1968), p. 116.

2. J. Krishnamurti, *Freedom From the Known* (New York, NY: Harper and Row, 1969), pp. 105-6.

3. Annie Kirkwood, *Mary's Message of Hope* (Blue Dolphin Publishing Co., 1995), pp. 8-10.

4.   M.C., *Light On The Path* (Los Angeles, CA: Theosophy Company, 1975).

5.   Matthew Fox, The *Coming of the Cosmic Christ* (San Francisco, CA: Harper & Row, Publishers, 1988), pp. 59-60.

6.   Emmanuel Swedenborg, clairvoyant who journeyed through space. Translated by Dr. George Dole, *Heaven and Hell* (Swedenborg Foundation, Inc., 1984), pp. 170, 178-179.

7.   *A Course in Miracles* (Foundation for Inner Peace, 1975), Text p. 614.

BIBLIOGRAPHY

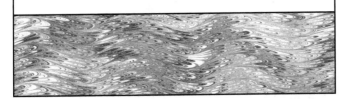

A Course In Miracles. Foundation for Inner Peace, 1975.

Andrews, Ted. *How to Meet and Work with Spirit Guides*. Llewellyn Publications, 1994.

Bach, Edward, M.D. *The Bach Flower Remedies*. Keats Publishing, Inc., 1979.

Baldwin, William J. *Spirit Releasement Therapy*. The Human Potential Foundation Press, Second Edition, 1993.

Burnham, Sophy. *A Book of Angels*. Ballantine Books, 1990.

Burns, Barbara. *Channeling*. Light Technology Publishing, 1992.

Carey, Ken. *The Starseed Transmissions*. Harper Collins Publishers, 1982.

Castaneda, Carlos. *The Power of Silence*. Simon & Schuster, 1987.

Chopra, Deepak, M.D. *Ageless Body, Timeless Mind*. Harmony Books, 1993.

Chopra, Deepak, M.D. *Perfect Health*. Harmony Books, 1991.

Chopra, Deepak, M.D. *Quantam Healing*. Bantam Books, 1989.

Cooke, Grace. *Meditation*. White Eagle Publishing Trust, 1955.

Cunningham, Donna. *Flower Remedies Handbook*. Sterling Publishing Company, 1992.

Daniel, Alma; Wyllie, Timothy; and Ramer, Andrew. *Ask Your Angels*. Ballantine Books, 1992.

Davidson, Gustav. *A Dictionary of Angels*. The Free Press, A Division of Macmillan, Inc., 1971.

Dossey, Larry, M.D. *Healing Words*. Harper Collins Publishers, 1993.

Ebon, Martin. *True Experiences in Communicating With The Dead*. Garrett Publications, 1959.

Essene, Virginia and Nidle, Sheldon. *You Are Becoming A Galactic Human*. S.E.E. Publishing Company, 1994.

Fiore, Dr. Edith. *The Unquiet Dead*. Ballantine Books, 1988.

The Findhorn Community. *The Findhorn Garden*. Harper & Row, 1975.

Fox, Matthew. *Original Blessing*. Bear & Company, 1983.

Fox, Matthew. *The Coming of the Cosmic Christ*. Harper & Row, 1988.

Frissell, Bob. *Nothing In This Book Is True, But It's Exactly How Things Are*. Frog, Ltd., 1994.

Francis, Fr. Thomas, O.C.S.O. *Angels*. Holy Spirit Monastery.

Gidel, Robert D. and Bostwick, Kathryn B. *So You Can't Believe You're Dead?* Andaraeon Foundation, Inc. 1993.

Goldman, Karen. *The Angel Book*. Simon & Schuster, 1992.

Goldsmith, Joel S. *The Art of Meditation*. Harper Collins Publishers, 1956.

Graham, Billy. *Angels — God's Secret Agents*. World Publishing, 1975.

Hawken, Paul. *The Magic of Findhorn*. Bantam Books, 1976.

Hay, Louise L. *Heal Your Body*. Hay House, 1996.

Hickman, Irene, D.O. *Remote Depossession*. Hickman Systems, 1994.

Hodson, Geoffrey. *Fairies at Work and at Play*. The Theosophical Publishing House, 1982.

Hodson, Geoffrey. *The Brotherhood of Angels and Men*. The Theosophical Publishing House, 1982.

Michael, E.J. *Queen of the Sun*. Mountain Rose Publishing, 1994.

Howard, Jane M. *Commune With The Angels*. A.R.E. Press, 1992.

Ingerman, Sandra. *Soul Retrieval*. Harper San Francisco, 1991.

Jampolsky, Gerald G. *Love is Letting Go of Fear*. Celestial Arts, 1979.

Kirkwood, Annie. *Mary's Message To the World*. Blue Dolphin Publishing, Inc., 1991.

Kirkwood, Annie. *Mary's Message Of Hope*. Blue Dolphin Publishing, Inc., 1995.

Kowalski, Gary. *The Souls of Animals*. Stillpoint Publishing, 1991.

Kryon. *The End Times*. The Kryon Writings, 1992.

Kryon. *Don't Think Like A Human: Book II*. The Kryon Writings, 1994.

Kryon. *Alchemy Of The Human Spirit: Book III*. The Kryon Writings, 1994.

Langlois, Carole Sanborn. *Soul Rescue — Help On the Way Home to Spirit*. That's The Spirit Publishing Company, 1993.

Loehr, Rev. Franklin. *Power of Prayer on Plants*. New American Library, 1969.

M.C. *Light On The Path*. Theosophy Company, 1975.

Marciniak, Barbara. *Bringers of the Dawn*. Bear & Company Publishing, 1992.

Martin, Jennifer and Dean, Rosemary. *The Angels Speak*. Prairie Angel Press, 1995.

Martin, Malachi. *Hostage to the Devil*. Harper San Francisco, 1992.

Maurey, Eugene. *Exorcism*. Whitford Press, 1988.

Meek, George W. *After We Die, What Then?* Ariel Press, 1987.

Merton, Thomas. *Contemplative Prayer*. Image Books, A Division of Doubleday & Company, Inc., 1971.

Montgomery, John Warwick. *Principalities and Powers*. Pyramid Publications, 1975.

Montgomery, Ruth. *A World Beyond*. Ballantine Books, 1971.

Morse, Melvin, M.D. *Gardening with Angels, Devas & Fairies*. In *Angel Times*, Angelic Realms Unlimited, Inc., 1995.

The New American Bible. St. Joseph Edition.

Newhouse, Flower A. *Rediscovering The Angels*. The Christward Ministry, 1976.

Pennington, M. Basil. *Centering Prayer*. Doubleday, Division of Bantam Doubleday Dell Publishing Group, Inc., 1980.

Petrak, Joyce, D.C.H. *How To Remember Bach Flower Remedies*. Curry-Peterson Press, 1991.

Prather, Hugh. *Notes To Myself*. Bantam Books, 1970.

Ritchie, George G., M.D. *Return From Tomorrow*. Baker Book House Company, 1978.

Scheffer, Victor B. *The Year of the Whale*. Charles Scribner's Sons, 1969.

Sheehan, Molly. *Flower Essences — A Guide to Green Hope Farm*. Green Hope Farm, 1994.

Skutch, Robert. *Journey Without Distance*. Celestial Arts, 1984.

Starr, Aloa. *Prisoners of Earth*. Light Technology, 1993.

Suenens, Cardinal Leon-Joseph. *Renewal and the Powers of Darkness*. Servant Books, 1983.

Sun Bear with Wabun Wind. *Black Dawn, Bright Day*. Simon & Schuster, 1992.

Swedenborg, Emmanuel. *Heaven and Hell*. Swedenborg Foundation, Inc., 1976.

Taylor, Terry Lynn. *Guardians of Hope*. H.J. Kramer, Inc., 1992.

Taylor, Terry Lynn. *Messengers of Light* H.J. Kramer, Inc., 1990.

Tompkins, Peter and Bird, Christopher. *Secret Life of Plants*. Avon Books, 1973.

White Eagle. *Spiritual Unfoldment 2*. White Eagle Publishing Trust, 1969.

Wilkerson, Ralph. *Beyond and Back*. Bantam Books, Inc., 1977.

Wright, Machaelle Small. *Behaving as if the God in All Life Mattered*. Perelandra, Ltd., 1987.

Wyllie, Timothy. *Dolphins, ETs and Angels*. Bear & Company, 1992.

Request for Information to Obtain a Remote Spirit Releasement

Therapists from the Natural Learning Center are available to assist clients.

To obtain detailed information, charges and a request form, send a stamped, self-addressed business-size envelope to:

Dr. Joyce Petrak
Natural Learning Center, Inc.
P.O. Box No. 839
Lenoir City, TN 37771

Please enclose a note requesting information for Remote Depossession (Spirit Releasement). This can be for yourself or another person you wish to help.

PLEASE, PLEASE CLEARLY PRINT *or type your name and address on the envelope to be returned to you. The Post Office returns illegibly written addresses.*

The Author — "Dr. Joy"

*D*r. Joyce Petrak *has been a* Holistic Health Practitioner since 1978 when she graduated as an Iridologist and Naturopathic Nutritional Consultant. Previously, she had received a Bachelor's Degree from the University of Detroit in Journalism and English and spent some years as a writer, editor and teacher.

Always taking more classes or seminars, in 1980 she took a course in Bach Flower Remedies and also went to a week-end seminar for *A Course in Miracles* (ACIM). She feels these two have made dramatic changes in her life. The Remedies are flower essences which help balance emotions and bring about a positive state. ACIM is a spiritually-based self-improvement study which aims at developing inner peace.

Always enthusiastic, she eventually began teaching Bach classes and wrote a text which differentiates the 38 Remedies and made classes fun by including a cartoon for each Remedy. (*How To Remember Bach Flower Remedies or… First, Get The Elephant Off Your Foot* is going into its third printing.)

In 1988 she took Dr. Bill Baldwin's *Spirit Releasement* course. Already a hypnotist, she added this work to her practice and soon it became her main focus. This book is one result.

She continued deeper studies into the mind and the subconscious and in 1991 received a doctorate in Clinical Hypnotherapy. Now, as "Dr. Joy," she sees clients, writes, lectures and teaches in various states.

She is a member of the International Medical and Dental Hypnotherapy Association (IMDHA), the Society for the Advancement of Natural Teachings (SANT), The Knoxville Writers' Group, the American Business Women (ABW) and Co-op American. With her husband, Robert, they are facilitators for an ACIM study group. They have four adult children and one grandchild.